The History of Psychology

Crafted by Skriuwer

Copyright © 2024 by Skriuwer.

All rights reserved. No part of this book may be used or reproduced in any form whatsoever without written permission except in the case of brief quotations in critical articles or reviews.

At **Skriuwer**, we're more than just a team—we're a global community of people who love books. In Frisian, "Skriuwer" means "writer," and that's at the heart of what we do: creating and sharing books with readers worldwide. Wherever you are in the world, **Skriuwer** is here to inspire learning.

Frisian is one of the oldest languages in Europe, closely related to English and Dutch, and is spoken by about **500,000 people** in the province of **Friesland** (Fryslân), located in the northern Netherlands. It's the second official language of the Netherlands, but like many minority languages, Frisian faces the challenge of survival in a modern, globalized world.

We're using the money we earn to promote the Frisian language.

For more information, contact : **kontakt@skriuwer.com** (www.skriuwer.com)

Table of Contents

Chapter 1: Introduction – Defining Psychology Across Time

- *Explains How The Concept Of "Psychology" Evolved Over Centuries.*
- *Sets The Stage For Understanding Why Historical Developments Matter.*
- *Highlights Early Observations Of Mental Processes Before Formal Science.*

Chapter 2: Prehistoric And Early Civilizations – Tracing The Earliest Ideas

- *Explores Prehistoric Beliefs About Mind And Behavior.*
- *Discusses Mesopotamian, Egyptian, And Other Early Approaches To Mental Health.*
- *Examines Rituals, Shamans, And The First Hints Of Psychological Insight.*

Chapter 3: Ancient Greece

- *Introduces Greek Speculation On Knowledge, Reality, And Human Nature.*
- *Profiles Pre-Socratics, Socrates, And Plato's Major Contributions.*
- *Shows How Philosophical Debates Laid Groundwork For Western Thought.*

Chapter 4: Aristotle And Hellenistic Psychology

- *Focuses On Aristotle's Comprehensive View Of The Soul And Faculties.*
- *Highlights Hellenistic Schools Like Stoicism And Epicureanism.*
- *Explores How Emotion And Logic Were Integrated Into Broader Philosophy.*

Chapter 5: The Roman Era And Early Christian Influences

- *Covers Roman Adaptations Of Greek Ideas (E.G., Galen's Physiology).*
- *Shows How Early Christian Thought Merged Philosophical And Spiritual Views.*
- *Examines Tensions Between Religious Doctrines And Natural Explanations.*

Chapter 6: The Middle Ages In Europe

- *Highlights The Scholastic Method In Medieval Universities.*
- *Explains How Aristotle's Works Were Preserved And Commented Upon.*
- *Shows Interplay Of Theology And Philosophical Speculation About The Soul.*

Chapter 7: The Islamic Golden Age

- *Details How Islamic Scholars Translated And Built On Greek Texts.*
- *Covers Avicenna, Al-Kindi, And Their Contributions To Mind And Health.*
- *Examines The Fusion Of Medicine, Philosophy, And Theological Perspectives.*

Chapter 8: The Renaissance And Humanism

- *Describes Renewed Focus On Individual Potential And Classical Learning.*
- *Shows How Art, Science, And Philosophy Intertwined In Renaissance Culture.*
- *Lays Groundwork For Empirical Approaches To Studying The Mind.*

Chapter 9: The Age Of Enlightenment And Empiricism

- Explores Bacon's Inductive Method And The Emergence Of Empirical Thought.
- Discusses How Reason, Observation, And Skepticism Challenged Old Dogmas.
- Paves The Way For Experimental Methods In Investigating Mental Processes.

Chapter 10: Early Modern Philosophers

- Covers Descartes' Dualism And Rationalist Stance.
- Highlights Locke's Empiricism And The "Blank Slate" Mind.
- Shows Hume's Skepticism About Causation And The Self.

Chapter 11: Transition To Scientific Psychology

- Details How Psychophysics And Physiology Bridged Philosophical Speculation With Data.
- Covers Early Reaction-Time Studies And Systematic Measurement Of Perception.
- Sets The Foundation For Psychology's Emergence As A Distinct Science.

Chapter 12: Wilhelm Wundt And The First Laboratories

- Profiles Wundt's Lab In Leipzig (1879) And Introspective Methods.
- Discusses The Structure Of Consciousness Approach And The Spread Of Labs Worldwide.
- Explains How Wundt's Influence Defined The New Discipline's Academic Identity.

Chapter 13: Structuralism And Edward Titchener

- Focuses On Titchener's Introspective Methodology And "Stimulus Error."
- Aims To Break Consciousness Into Sensations, Images, And Affections.
- Examines Critiques And The Eventual Decline Of Structuralism.

Chapter 14: William James And Functionalism

- Covers James's "Stream Of Consciousness" And Pragmatic Viewpoint.
- Shows How Functionalism Emphasized Adaptation, Function, And Real-World Use.
- Influenced American Psychology's Focus On Educational, Social, And Applied Topics.

Chapter 15: Psychoanalysis

- Explores Freud's Ideas On The Unconscious, Psychosexual Stages, And Dream Analysis.
- Shows How Jung And Adler Diverged, Developing Analytical And Individual Psychology.
- Highlights Psychoanalysis' Clinical Practice And Cultural Impact.

Chapter 16: Early Behaviorism

- Explains Thorndike's Trial-And-Error Learning (Law Of Effect).
- Covers Pavlov's Classical Conditioning And Reflexes.
- Presents Watson's Manifesto Rejecting Mental States, Focusing On Observable S-R.

Chapter 17: Behaviorism Under B.F. Skinner

- Centers On Operant Conditioning, Reinforcement, Punishment, And Shaping.
- Describes The Skinner Box And Schedules Of Reinforcement.
- Introduces Skinner's Radical Behaviorism And Broader Social/Educational Applications.

Chapter 18: Gestalt Psychology

- Highlights Holistic Perception Concepts And Laws (Figure-Ground, Closure, Etc.).
- Shows Köhler's Insight Learning In Apes, Challenging Simple S-R Views.
- Explores How Gestalt Ideas Contrasted With Behaviorism And Influenced Cognition.

Chapter 19: Early 20th Century Debates And Developments

- Reviews Clashes Between Behaviorism, Psychoanalysis, Gestalt, And Remaining Structuralists.
- Covers The Rise Of Mental Testing, Child Guidance, And Industrial Psychology.
- Shows How The Field Expanded Into Personality, Social Psychology, And Varied Applications.

Chapter 20: Bridging To The Mid-20th Century

- Summarizes Psychology's Status On The Eve Of World War Ii.
- Points To Emerging Trends (Cognitive Inferences, Deeper Social Applications).
- Marks A Transition Toward Mid-20th-Century Transformations And The Next Waves Of Theoretical Change.

CHAPTER 1: INTRODUCTION - DEFINING PSYCHOLOGY ACROSS TIME

1.1. Understanding the Meaning of "Psychology" in Historical Context

Psychology, in the simplest sense, is the systematic study of the mind and behavior. Yet, if we look at the term historically, it meant different things in different periods. Words like "mind," "psyche," and "soul" have shifted in meaning based on cultural norms, philosophical traditions, religious beliefs, and scientific approaches of the time. Long ago, there was no unified field called "psychology." Instead, there were many speculations and observations about what drives human thought, emotion, and action. These took shape in religious teachings, philosophical debates, and even in everyday attempts to understand why people do what they do.

Because the word "psychology" comes from Greek roots—psyche (meaning "soul" or "breath") and logos (meaning "word," "reason," or "study")—it is closely tied to ancient philosophical ideas. Over thousands of years, these ideas have changed. Early views involved supernatural causes or spiritual explanations, while later approaches focused on natural and rational perspectives. In ancient times, it was normal to discuss the mind in terms of a soul, spirit, or life force. People thought behaviors and mental states came from gods, demons, or cosmic forces. Meanwhile, philosophers grappled with questions about the nature of knowledge, truth, and reality, all of which shaped how we view human thought.

In modern usage, psychology is recognized as a scientific discipline that uses systematic methods like observation, experimentation, and measurement to reach conclusions. But in this book, we will not delve into contemporary methods. Instead, we will focus on how the discipline emerged over centuries. We will see how the development of psychology as a distinct science was slow, influenced by historical context. Ideas built upon each other. Philosophers, physicians, theologians, and even laypeople all contributed in some way to our evolving concepts of the mind.

1.2. The Importance of Studying Psychology's Past

It might seem outdated to learn what people once believed about the mind and behavior, especially if those beliefs have been replaced by newer findings. However, understanding the history of psychology is not just about memorizing old theories. Instead, it gives us a sense of how knowledge develops over time and how certain methods or biases shape our understanding of human nature.

In many fields, including physics or biology, early theories can seem quite strange compared to modern knowledge. The same is true in psychology. People used to rely on introspection, spiritual or religious perspectives, or anecdotal observations without what we might consider rigorous scientific methods. Yet these older viewpoints often contained seeds of truth or at least asked useful questions. By seeing which ideas survived, evolved, or were discarded, we can better appreciate how we arrived at certain foundations of thought.

Moreover, the history of psychology shows how it did not appear out of nowhere. Its roots in philosophy, biology, medicine, and even theology highlight the interdisciplinary nature of questions about mind and behavior. For instance, if we look at historical debates about free will or determinism, we see they echo through centuries. The same goes for discussions of nature versus nurture, or the relationship between the mind and the body. These are issues that first appeared in the works of ancient philosophers and religious writers.

1.3. Early Observations on Mind and Behavior

Long before formal records of philosophical inquiry, people made assumptions about how the mind worked based on survival. If a tribe member acted in ways that harmed the group, the community might interpret that as a curse or possession by spirits. Dreams were often seen as messages from another realm, hinting that mental activity continued even when the body was at rest. This shows that even at the very dawn of civilization, people recognized that thought and behavior had deeper layers than simple reflexes.

The earliest attempts to treat mental or behavioral issues often involved shamans, spiritual leaders, or medicine men who used rituals to address what they believed were supernatural causes of distress. Though not scientific in the modern sense, these practices were the beginnings of attempts to categorize and manage unusual mental states. Over time, some practical observations got passed down through oral traditions, forming the foundation for future theories.

1.4. Linking Psychology to Broader Intellectual Traditions

As societies became more complex, questions about the human mind started to overlap with broader intellectual traditions. In the West, for example, ancient Greek philosophers like Plato and Aristotle wrestled with the nature of knowledge, reality, and virtue. Their ideas about reason, emotion, and consciousness influenced not just later thinkers in Greece and Rome but also the early Christian theologians of the medieval period.

In the East, major religious and philosophical systems like Hinduism, Buddhism, and Confucianism also presented ideas about the mind, suffering, the self, and how to attain inner peace. Although we often categorize these beliefs under religion or spirituality, many of them contain psychological insights about how humans think, feel, and act.

Because this book focuses primarily on Western psychology's roots, we will see how that specific tradition went from mythological explanations to philosophical reflection. Then it was shaped by Roman and early Christian thinkers, carried forward through the Middle Ages, and reborn during the Renaissance. It eventually led to the Enlightenment and paved the way for the first attempts to make psychology an experimental science. However, we will also note the key contributions of Middle Eastern scholars who preserved and advanced Greek texts, preventing them from being lost, as well as how these texts later re-entered Europe.

1.5. Transition from Philosophy to Systematic Study

One of the most important themes in the history of psychology is the gradual shift from purely philosophical speculation—where someone might ponder the nature of the soul or whether knowledge is innate—to systematic investigation using empirical methods. In early eras, measurement tools were scarce, so philosophers relied on logic or introspection.

Over time, as the natural sciences advanced in areas like astronomy, physics, and chemistry, people began thinking about ways to measure or observe mental processes more carefully. This was a slow process. It needed instruments, methods, and a belief that the mind could be studied in a systematic manner just like one might study plants or planets.

A major turning point came in the 19th century when scholars such as Wilhelm Wundt set up the first laboratory dedicated to psychological research. Instead of purely debating philosophical ideas, they started conducting experiments, measuring reaction times, and gathering data in a controlled environment. This laid the foundation for the discipline as a field in its own right.

But this did not happen in isolation. Scientists who studied sensory perception (psychophysics) helped make the case that mental events could be measured. Philosophers like John Locke and David Hume argued that the mind was shaped by experience, thus paving the way for empirical methods. Meanwhile, figures like René Descartes pushed forward the concept that mind and body could be studied separately, fueling debates about the nature of consciousness and material existence.

1.6. Reasons for Excluding Modern Developments from This Book

In a typical survey of psychology, one might jump from Wundt to major 20th-century theories like Behaviorism, Psychoanalysis, or Humanism, and then proceed to modern techniques involving brain scans. But our purpose here is to stay rooted in history—mainly up until the early to mid-20th century. Modern developments like neuroscience, cognitive science, and advanced therapies, while important, are outside our scope.

By focusing on earlier periods, we can carefully trace how each idea emerged and how it built upon or replaced previous views. We can see the key transitions from religious to philosophical explanations, from philosophical speculation to more systematic observations, and finally from a broad approach to a more specialized, experimental discipline. This historical focus helps clarify the path psychology followed without the confusion of jumping into modern controversies or findings.

1.7. The Plan for This Book

This book is structured chronologically, beginning with prehistoric times and the earliest civilizations, then moving through ancient Greece, the Roman era, the Middle Ages, the Islamic Golden Age, the Renaissance, the Enlightenment, and so forth. We will examine major figures like Plato, Aristotle, Galen, Avicenna, Aquinas, Descartes, Locke, Hume, Kant, Wundt, William James, Sigmund Freud, and others who played key roles in shaping the study of the mind.

We will see how schools of thought rose, fell, and sometimes returned in new forms. For example, the debate between rationalism and empiricism reappears throughout history, each time informed by different cultural and intellectual climates. We will also study how different societies interpreted mental phenomena, whether through a spiritual lens or a naturalistic one, and how these interpretations affected people's lives.

Every chapter focuses on a specific historical period or key transition. We will try to capture the essence of each era, highlight important individuals and texts, and discuss the influence of major events like the fall of the Roman Empire or the rise of universities in the Middle Ages. In doing so, we aim to present a clear picture of how psychology's early story unfolded.

1.8. Early Definitions of "Mind," "Soul," and "Spirit"

A core concept in psychology is the "mind." But in many ancient cultures, this idea was blurred with notions of a "soul" or "spirit." Sometimes, these were viewed as immortal entities that left the body after death. Sometimes, they were believed to be material substances like "breath" or "heat" that animated the physical body. Even the root of the English word "spirit" comes from the Latin "spiritus," meaning breath.

Because older languages often lacked a separate term for mental activity, many ancient texts that discuss mental processes do so in a spiritual or religious way. For instance, early Hebrew texts refer to the "heart" as the seat of emotion and thought. The ancient Egyptians believed in multiple components of the soul—each playing a different role in a person's life and afterlife. Meanwhile, Greek philosophers started to dissect these concepts in more analytical terms, asking questions like: Is the mind separate from the body? Is it divine, or purely natural?

1.9. The Interplay of Religion and Philosophy

Religion played a major role in shaping thoughts about human nature. In many historical periods, religious institutions were the main centers of learning and authority. Questions about the mind were often explored within theological frameworks. This meant that if a person wanted to propose a new theory about the soul or consciousness, they had to ensure it did not conflict with the dominant religious teachings of the time.

The Middle Ages in Europe, for example, were dominated by Christian Scholasticism. Monasteries and cathedral schools became the repositories of knowledge. Thinkers like Thomas Aquinas blended Aristotelian philosophy with Christian doctrine. Although theology was the "queen of the sciences," many commentaries on Aristotle touched upon psychological topics like memory, perception, and will. Even though the approach was religious, it preserved a lot of philosophical knowledge and passed it down through centuries.

1.10. Preserving Knowledge Through Translation

A crucial aspect of psychology's history involves the preservation of ancient texts. When the Western Roman Empire fell, much of the knowledge of Greek and Roman philosophers risked being lost. Meanwhile, the Eastern Roman Empire continued in Byzantium (Constantinople), and scholars in the Islamic world translated Greek works into Arabic. They also wrote commentaries, making their own breakthroughs in medicine and philosophy. Later, these Arabic texts were translated into Latin and brought to medieval Europe, sparking renewed interest in ancient thought.

This chain of translation and commentary affected psychology by ensuring that the works of Aristotle, Galen, and others survived. Had these texts been lost, the history of psychology might have followed a different path. The debates we see in later medieval universities often stem from close readings of these ancient authors. The thirst for knowledge about the human mind was kept alive because people had access to these earlier works in some form.

1.11. The Role of Observation and Experimentation

Before the emergence of formal scientific psychology, people relied on basic observation and inference. For example, they noticed that certain herbs or environments seemed to help people who were distressed. They recognized patterns in how children learn or how adults respond to fear. Over time, some began taking notes or recording these observations in medical treatises.

Yet true experimentation—where you systematically vary one factor and keep others constant to see its effect—was rare in the ancient and medieval periods. A few exceptions can be found in areas like optics or physiology, but applying such methods to the mind was not common. Many believed that studying the mind required introspection or theological reflection, not physical experiments.

That began to change as we move closer to the Renaissance and Enlightenment. Thinkers like Francis Bacon argued for an empirical approach to all areas of knowledge, including the study of human nature. Slowly, this mindset created room for more systematic studies. Physicians who studied the brain and nerves also contributed, suggesting that mental processes might have physical correlates—an idea that gained more traction over time.

1.12. From Speculation to Questions of Proof

In the ancient world, a statement about the mind could be accepted if it came from a respected authority or if it aligned with established religious or philosophical doctrine. Over centuries, however, the demand for "proof" grew. This shift was part of the larger movement toward scientific thinking that included the works of Copernicus,

Galileo, and others who challenged traditional beliefs by using systematic observation and mathematics.

For psychology, the process was slower and more complicated. The human mind does not present itself as easily to measurement as physical objects. Early attempts at "proving" theories about mental states were limited by the available tools. When instruments like chronometers, tuning forks, and later advanced devices appeared, researchers began measuring reaction times, thresholds of perception, and so forth. This will come into sharper focus in later chapters, especially when we discuss the 19th-century push toward experimental methods.

1.13. A Bridge Between Science and the Humanities

Psychology's history also shows how the field has always existed at the edge between science and the humanities. Ancient philosophers debated moral questions, the nature of happiness, and what it means to be virtuous. These are areas we might now associate with ethics or philosophy. But they also looked at emotion, reason, and decision-making processes—topics that lie at the heart of psychology.

Because of this blend, the early story of psychology often intersects with literature, theology, art, and medicine. For instance, the literary works of ancient poets can reveal how a culture viewed mental states like love, despair, or madness. Medical texts of Greek or Roman origin show how doctors understood the relationship between bodily fluids and temperament. This interplay highlights why psychology never developed in isolation; it drew on multiple sources of knowledge.

1.14. Toward the Formalization of Thought

In ancient Mesopotamia or Egypt, knowledge was not separated into neat disciplines. People concerned themselves with managing day-to-day life, interpreting omens, or healing diseases. Over time, "natural philosophy" emerged as a broad umbrella that tried to explain reality through observation and reasoning.

Psychology, as part of natural philosophy, was entangled with other inquiries about physics, biology, or astronomy. But as philosophical traditions evolved, people began to see specific areas of focus. Some thinkers specialized in logic, others in ethics, some in metaphysics, and still others in what we might call "the philosophy of mind." This differentiation laid the groundwork for the eventual separation of psychology from philosophy.

1.15. Why the Timeline Matters

It might be easy to assume that ideas about the human mind progressed in a straight line—starting from superstition, evolving into philosophical thought, and finally leading to scientific practice. However, history rarely progresses so cleanly. There were periods in which old ideas reappeared in new forms. For instance, the Renaissance revived ancient Greek and Roman concepts that had gone out of favor in medieval Europe.

Some eras emphasized religious interpretations of the mind. Others turned toward logic and rationality. Sometimes, both existed side by side, influencing each other in complex ways. By taking a chapter-by-chapter approach through different historical stages, we can appreciate these complexities.

1.16. Anticipating Key Questions in Psychology's Early History

Before we move forward, it is helpful to highlight a few timeless questions that will appear throughout the historical record:

1. **Nature vs. Nurture:** Are our thoughts and behaviors more influenced by biology or by experience?
2. **Mind-Body Problem:** Is the mind separate from the body, or is it merely an aspect of physical processes?
3. **Origins of Knowledge:** Do we come into the world with innate ideas, or do we learn everything through our senses?
4. **Rationality vs. Emotion:** How do logic and feeling interact in human decision-making and behavior?
5. **Psychological Health and Illness:** What causes mental distress, and how can it be addressed or healed?

These questions were not formulated exactly in these terms in ancient times, but variations of them appear in old myths, philosophical dialogues, and religious doctrines. By noticing these recurring themes, we can see how psychology's core puzzles are deeply rooted in human curiosity about ourselves.

CHAPTER 2: PREHISTORIC AND EARLY CIVILIZATIONS: TRACING THE EARLIEST IDEAS

2.1. Life Before Written Records

When we think about the history of psychology, we might imagine Greek philosophers or medieval theologians. Yet, long before written records, people formed ideas about why humans think, feel, and behave in certain ways. In these prehistoric times, there is no direct documentation of what people believed about the mind. However, we can glean hints from archaeological findings like cave paintings, burial sites, and artifacts that suggest some understanding of mental processes, emotional states, and spiritual beliefs.

For example, consider cave paintings found in places like Lascaux in France or Altamira in Spain. These paintings often show animals and hunting scenes, which might indicate attempts to influence reality through symbolic representation. Some experts argue that these artworks could have been part of rituals meant to ensure success in the hunt, reflecting the human desire to shape outcomes by tapping into spiritual or mental realms. Although this is speculation, it suggests a belief that the mind or spirit could affect the physical world.

We can also look at burial customs. The care with which prehistoric communities sometimes buried their dead—placing tools, ornaments, or food alongside the body—points to beliefs about an afterlife, a soul, or at least a continuation of existence beyond physical death. This is not "psychology" in the modern sense, but it does show that people recognized something beyond mere physical existence. They must have had concepts about memory, spirit, or consciousness that continued even when the body ceased to function.

2.2. The Role of Shamans and Spiritual Leaders

In many hunter-gatherer societies and early agricultural communities, shamans or spiritual leaders served as guides not only in religious matters but also in what we might call mental health. They used rituals, chants, or hallucinogenic substances to enter altered states of consciousness. By doing so, they believed they could communicate with spirits, heal sickness, and solve communal problems.

Such practices indicate a recognition that states of mind could vary widely—from ordinary wakefulness to trance-like conditions. The existence of these specialized roles suggests that people sought ways to address unusual behaviors or experiences. If a member of the tribe was behaving erratically, the community might view it as a spiritual crisis rather than a biological or "psychological" one in our modern terms. The solution involved ceremonies aimed at restoring balance or driving out harmful spirits.

While these methods do not align with scientific psychology, they show that people were actively trying to explain and influence mental states. They also reflect the strong link between mental phenomena and spiritual beliefs in early human societies.

2.3. The Dawn of Civilization: Mesopotamia

Many scholars consider Mesopotamia—often called the "cradle of civilization"—as one of the earliest regions to develop complex societies. Located in the fertile valleys of the Tigris and Euphrates

Rivers, Mesopotamian city-states, such as Sumer, Akkad, Babylon, and Assyria, left us some of the earliest written records on clay tablets.

Although these records focus heavily on administrative, legal, and religious matters, we can find glimpses of how these people thought about the mind. For instance, the Mesopotamians had deities responsible for various aspects of life, including health and illness. They viewed diseases—physical or mental—as punishments from gods or as the work of evil spirits. Healers performed rituals and made offerings to appease these deities or drive away malevolent forces.

The "mind" was not a term they separated out the way we do today. Rather, they might talk about a person's "heart" or "liver" as the center of emotion or decision-making. They believed the liver, for instance, was key to certain emotional states because they noticed it was a vital organ. The Mesopotamians also produced early medical texts that included symptoms of conditions we might now label as forms of mental distress. Their approach to diagnosing and treating these conditions combined incantations, herbal remedies, and spiritual guidance.

2.4. Ancient Egypt and the Concept of the Soul

Ancient Egypt had a deep concern with the afterlife and the soul. Egyptians believed in several components of a person's being, such as the Ka (life force), the Ba (personality or individual essence), and the Akh (a transformed spirit after death). Mummification practices were designed to preserve the body so these spiritual elements could function in the afterlife.

Their beliefs about the soul were tied to moral and ethical behavior. The "Weighing of the Heart" ceremony in the Book of the Dead shows the idea that a person's heart would be weighed against a feather to determine purity. If the heart was heavier, filled with wrongdoing, the person's soul would face negative consequences. This can be seen as an early link between moral conduct and the "health" or condition of one's spiritual essence.

Though we cannot directly say the Egyptians had a formal psychology, they did think about behavior, moral choice, and an internal essence that governed one's fate in this life and the next. They also recognized psychosomatic connections. Some medical papyri, such as the Ebers Papyrus, discuss conditions that might be partly mental, though they usually framed them in spiritual terms.

2.5. Early Explanations of Dreams

Dreams have fascinated humans across all cultures and historical periods. In Mesopotamia, dream interpretation was a specialized skill. People believed gods communicated through dreams, sending messages or omens. Egyptian records also show an interest in dream interpretation, often linking dreams to divine or demonic influences.

These beliefs imply that ancient peoples recognized that the mind continues to operate in some way during sleep, generating images and experiences that can have personal or communal significance. People often consulted priests or oracles to interpret their dreams, hoping to gain insight into personal decisions, upcoming dangers, or spiritual matters. In a sense, this is an early form of "psychological" interpretation, albeit grounded in supernatural frameworks.

2.6. Approaches to Behavioral Deviance in Early Civilizations

Even in the earliest civilizations, social norms and laws controlled how people behaved. When someone's actions fell outside what was considered acceptable, the community or its authorities took note. In Sumerian or Babylonian law codes, there were punishments for harming others, stealing, or committing other crimes, suggesting these societies had some sense of distinguishing typical from atypical behavior.

But what about mental disturbances? Without a modern concept of mental illness, many early texts describe unusual actions as demon possession or the result of gods' anger. Various clay tablets include spells and rituals intended to drive out whatever force was causing the strange behavior. Alternatively, if a person was seen as too disruptive or dangerous, physical punishments or social exclusion could follow.

Yet, there is some indication that not all treatments were harsh. In certain Egyptian or Mesopotamian texts, we find references to healing temples or quiet rooms where individuals could rest and be cared for by priests or healers. While the rationale behind this was spiritual, the outcome might sometimes have offered relief or comfort, at least temporarily.

2.7. The Emergence of Writing and Record Keeping

The development of writing systems in Mesopotamia (cuneiform) and Egypt (hieroglyphics) changed the way knowledge was stored and shared. It enabled more systematic record-keeping of observations, including those we might link to early psychology. Scribes could document rituals, healing practices, and the outcomes of certain interventions.

This did not lead directly to scientific methods, but it set a foundation for building a body of written knowledge that future generations could read, revise, or expand. Over time, writing also facilitated philosophical debate, since scholars could refer to older texts and argue with them in a structured manner.

2.8. Influence of Mythology on Psychology

Myths, which were plentiful in early civilizations, often personified psychological tendencies or states as gods or legendary heroes. In Mesopotamian mythology, the epic of Gilgamesh explores themes of friendship, the fear of death, and the pursuit of meaning—showing an awareness of deep emotional and existential questions. In Egyptian myths, gods like Isis, Osiris, and Set represent cycles of life, death, and rebirth, reflecting psychological experiences of loss and renewal.

While these myths are not "theories of psychology," they reveal how ancient people conceptualized internal conflicts, emotional struggles, and coping mechanisms. Characters in myths often undergo transformations, moral dilemmas, or crises of identity. These tales served as communal stories that could explain complex emotions and moral questions in a symbolic way.

2.9. The Transition to More Structured Thought

As civilizations like those in Mesopotamia and Egypt grew, they interacted with neighboring regions. This exchange of goods and ideas set the stage for more sophisticated reflections on the mind. The people who traveled or traded in these areas might share healing techniques, religious beliefs, or philosophical notions.

Over time, centers of learning emerged. In Egypt, for instance, the city of Heliopolis was known for its priests who studied astronomy, mathematics, and possibly early forms of medicine. In Mesopotamia, temples often had libraries of clay tablets. However, the knowledge in these places remained largely tied to religious or state functions.

Yet, these early foundations were essential. They influenced later cultures, like ancient Greece, which inherited many ideas about gods, spirits, and the nature of existence from older civilizations. Without Mesopotamia and Egypt, the Greek philosophers might not have had some of the background assumptions they took for granted.

2.10. Healing Practices and Proto-Medical Observations

Both Mesopotamians and Egyptians had proto-medical traditions. Although these were entangled with spiritual beliefs, they did include observation of symptoms and attempts at remedies. The Edwin Smith Papyrus from ancient Egypt, for example, outlines surgical procedures and notes on injuries, showing an early scientific approach to the body. While it mostly deals with physical wounds, it hints at how Egyptians began separating physical processes from purely spiritual matters.

Some of these medical texts also recorded cases of what we might today call depression or anxiety, though they were explained in terms of curses or the displeasure of gods. Treatments could involve both medicinal herbs and incantations. This dual approach reveals that people recognized something beyond the physical body was involved in these conditions.

2.11. Astrology and Cosmic Influences on Behavior

In Mesopotamia especially, astrology was a significant factor in explaining both personal and collective events. Observing the movements of stars and planets, Mesopotamian astrologers believed these celestial bodies influenced the fate of individuals and societies. People thought a person's mental state or personality could be affected by astral configurations.

While this might seem far from modern psychology, it was an early attempt to find patterns or causes for human behavior in a larger system. By linking events on Earth to celestial phenomena, they tried to impose order and predictability on human affairs. Although we do not consider astrology a science now, in ancient times it represented a type of systematic reasoning about correlations.

2.12. Moral and Ethical Considerations

Both Mesopotamian and Egyptian societies had moral codes. The famous Code of Hammurabi (Babylonian law) is one of the oldest deciphered writings of length in the world. It shows how justice and retribution were central concerns. Embedded within these laws is an assumption that people are responsible for their actions and that certain behaviors warrant certain punishments.

In a rudimentary way, this suggests a notion of accountability and volition: if a person commits a crime, it is because they chose to do so and should face the consequences. At the same time, if a person's actions were deemed the result of a demonic force, that might alter the approach. They might then require ritual cleansing instead of a legal sentence.

For Egypt, moral righteousness was key to achieving a good afterlife. Thus, Egyptians placed emphasis on honesty, kindness, and fulfilling religious duties. This moral framework shaped how they viewed individuals who behaved out of line. There was a psychological dimension here, since moral failing could be interpreted as a kind of internal imbalance that affected one's destiny.

2.13. Archeological Clues to Emotional Life

Beyond written texts, archaeology offers clues about emotions and interpersonal relationships in these early civilizations. Tomb inscriptions might contain expressions of grief or love. For instance, Egyptian inscriptions occasionally show spouses speaking affectionately about each other, or parents lamenting the death of a child. These reveal that the emotional life of ancient people, in many ways, was not so different from ours.

We also find evidence of celebrations, festivals, and rituals that likely served to build communal bonds and lift spirits. Music, dance, and communal feasting were common in ancient Mesopotamia and Egypt. These social activities could be seen as forms of emotional expression or stress relief. Though they did not label them as "psychological well-being," these cultural practices certainly had an impact on mental states.

2.14. Early Thoughts on Intelligence and Skill

When societies became more specialized, people noticed differences in skills and aptitudes. Certain individuals became scribes, a role requiring literacy and record-keeping abilities. Others specialized in building, agriculture, or leadership. Over time, it became clear that some people were more adept at learning complex tasks.

Although there was no concept of measuring intelligence with formal tools, there was recognition that not everyone had the same capacities. Apprenticeships might serve as a rudimentary form of "talent identification," where a master craftsman would select students who showed promise. In a way, this is an early acknowledgment that cognitive abilities vary among individuals.

2.15. Influence on Later Civilizations

Mesopotamian and Egyptian ideas spread across the ancient Near East and the Mediterranean, influencing Hebrew thought, and eventually Greek and Roman cultures. Even though the Greeks took a more explicit philosophical turn, many of their initial assumptions about divine influence, the soul, and the supernatural likely have indirect roots in these older civilizations.

For example, when the Greek historian Herodotus visited Egypt, he wrote about their customs and how they approached life and death. This kind of cross-cultural contact enriched Greek thought, which in turn formed the bedrock of much Western philosophy and science.

2.16. The Limitations of Early Concepts

While prehistoric and early civilizations laid important groundwork, their explanations of mental life were limited by the knowledge and technology of their time. They did not distinguish between physical and psychological causes in the way we do today. Everything was interwoven with religion, myth, and superstition. Illness, misfortune, or strange behavior could be attributed to spirits, gods, or cosmic shifts.

Nevertheless, the fact that they devised any system at all to interpret mental states, predict behavior, and propose remedies is significant. It shows that questions about the mind have existed as long as human culture has. People have always sought to understand and influence behavior, even if their methods and explanations were bound to their era's worldviews.

2.17. Seeds of Future Inquiry

In these ancient societies, certain observations hinted at future scientific principles. For instance, the way some Egyptian physicians carefully documented injuries to the head and changes in personality or behavior suggests an early recognition of the brain's importance. Mesopotamian texts that described different types of "madness" or anxiety laid the foundation for categorizing mental disturbances.

These seeds would later grow in Greek thought, where thinkers like Hippocrates started to propose naturalistic explanations for illness, including mental illness. The idea that what we call "psychological" could have physical or natural explanations—instead of being purely spiritual—emerges from these early roots.

CHAPTER 3: ANCIENT GREECE

3.1. The Intellectual Climate of Early Greece

When we move from the early civilizations of Mesopotamia and Egypt to ancient Greece, we see a major shift in how people sought explanations for the world. In Mesopotamia and Egypt, religion and mythology dominated daily life, and the supernatural was a primary explanation for events. While the Greeks had their gods and myths, some of their thinkers started looking for natural principles behind the phenomena they observed. This drive for rational inquiry laid the groundwork for Western philosophy and eventually shaped how we think about psychology.

By the time of the Pre-Socratic philosophers (roughly the 6th and 5th centuries BCE), Greece was not yet a unified country but a collection of city-states like Athens, Sparta, and others spread around the Aegean Sea. Travel and trade among these city-states and nearby civilizations allowed for the exchange of ideas. Because of this connectivity, radical new ways of thinking could spread more easily than in some older, more centralized empires.

The question "What is the world made of?" was central to early Greek thought, leading philosophers to propose basic substances or principles behind reality. While this might seem purely physical, it indirectly set the stage for thinking about human beings and their internal processes. If water or air was the fundamental substance of the universe, what did that mean for life, thought, or the soul? Such questions eventually inspired more direct examinations of the mind.

3.2. Moving from Myth to Reason

Before the Pre-Socratics, the Greeks relied on mythological explanations for natural and human phenomena. Gods like Zeus, Hera, and Apollo governed everything from weather patterns to personal fates. Epic poets such as Homer and Hesiod told stories that provided moral lessons, cultural unity, and a shared cosmology. However, beginning in the 6th century BCE, some thinkers started to propose that natural events did not necessarily stem from the gods but from rational, observable processes.

This transition from mythos to logos—myth to reason—was crucial. The Pre-Socratics did not reject the existence of the gods outright, but they reduced the gods' role in explaining physical processes. By seeking explanations in material or rational terms, they also laid the foundation for exploring the human mind in a more systematic way. If the cosmos could be understood through reason, perhaps human behavior, thought, and emotion could be approached similarly.

Yet, these early philosophers did not separate "psychology" from other areas of inquiry. Their studies encompassed what we might now call physics, biology, meteorology, and more. All of it was considered "philosophy" or "natural philosophy." Nonetheless, their emphasis on observation and rational argument was a profound shift that reverberates through the history of psychology.

3.3. The Milesian Thinkers

The city of Miletus on the Ionian coast of Asia Minor (modern-day Turkey) was home to some of the earliest Greek philosophers. Thales (c. 624–c. 546 BCE) is often credited with asserting that water was the fundamental substance from which all else emerged. This might sound simplistic now, but what matters is that Thales looked for a unifying principle in nature that wasn't a deity. By doing so, he implicitly encouraged thinking in terms of cause and effect within the natural world.

Anaximander (c. 610–c. 546 BCE), a student of Thales, introduced the concept of the "apeiron," or the "boundless," as the origin of all things. He speculated about evolution-like processes and suggested that humans might have come from fish-like creatures. While not directly addressing the mind, his ideas about natural processes shaping living beings could be seen as early attempts to explain human attributes, including cognition, without invoking supernatural forces.

Anaximenes (c. 586–c. 526 BCE) proposed that air (or "pneuma") was the fundamental substance. For him, the compression or rarefaction of air gave rise to everything else—clouds, water, earth, and so on. The notion that an invisible substance (like air) could form the basis of life nudged future thinkers to consider immaterial processes as important. Later philosophers would grapple with the "breath" or "spirit" as something that animates life, possibly influencing early notions of soul and mind.

3.4. Heraclitus and Parmenides

While the Milesians focused on identifying a single substance, other Pre-Socratic thinkers turned to questions of change, identity, and perception. Heraclitus of Ephesus (c. 535–c. 475 BCE) is famous for his assertion that "all things are in flux." He used the image of a river, claiming one cannot step into the same river twice because new waters are always flowing. This perspective emphasizes constant change and suggests that stability or permanence is an illusion.

Parmenides of Elea (5th century BCE) took the opposite stance. He argued that change is illusory, and reality is a single, unchanging substance. According to Parmenides, the senses deceive us. What seems like change is merely our flawed perception.

Both positions had implications for how the Greeks viewed the mind. If the world is constant flux (Heraclitus), how do we attain knowledge or hold on to a concept? Is the mind itself in a state of ongoing change? Conversely, if reality is unchanging (Parmenides), then are our mental experiences untrustworthy illusions? These concerns about perception and knowledge would become core psychological questions, though not yet named as such.

3.5. Pythagoras and the Early Concept of the Soul

Pythagoras (c. 570–c. 495 BCE) is well known for mathematical achievements, but he also founded a philosophical and religious community that profoundly influenced Greek thought. His followers believed in the transmigration of souls (reincarnation) and stressed the importance of living a disciplined life to purify the soul. For Pythagoras, numbers and mathematical relationships were the true essence of the cosmos, reflecting an orderly system hidden beneath appearances.

In Pythagorean thought, the soul was not merely a life force; it had a moral and intellectual dimension. This marks a step toward a more structured concept of the mind or psyche. Pythagoras and his followers associated certain mental states with bodily purity, diet, and ethical living. Their emphasis on inner purification and intellectual contemplation foreshadowed later philosophical schools that tied moral virtue to mental well-being.

3.6. The Sophists and the Focus on Human Affairs

As Greek civilization advanced in the 5th century BCE, Athens emerged as a cultural powerhouse. Teachers known as Sophists traveled from city to city, offering instruction in rhetoric, argumentation, and other subjects considered crucial for public life. Figures like Protagoras, Gorgias, and Hippias were famous for their ability to persuade and for their willingness to challenge conventional beliefs.

The Sophists shifted philosophical attention from the cosmos to human affairs. They asked questions like: What is virtue? How do we know what is just or unjust? Their interest in language and persuasion implies an early focus on cognition—how do people form beliefs, and how can those beliefs be influenced? While the Sophists were sometimes criticized for manipulating language without regard for truth, they undeniably pushed Greek thought toward issues of human psychology, ethics, and social behavior.

3.7. Socrates

Socrates (c. 470–399 BCE) did not leave behind any writings. We know his ideas primarily through the dialogues of his student, Plato. Socrates is famed for his assertion that "the unexamined life is not worth living," reflecting his belief that understanding oneself is crucial to a meaningful existence. He roamed the public spaces of Athens, asking probing questions—now known as the "Socratic method"—to expose contradictions in people's beliefs.

For Socrates, self-knowledge and virtue were intertwined. He believed that ignorance led to wrongdoing, suggesting a psychological link between knowledge and behavior. If a person truly understood goodness, they would act accordingly, implying that moral failings are the result of not truly knowing the good. This viewpoint connects epistemology (the theory of knowledge) with moral psychology.

While Socrates did not propose a detailed model of the mind, his relentless questioning technique emphasized critical reflection, a process that today might be considered a form of cognitive therapy in a loose sense. By challenging assumptions, Socrates aimed to lead his interlocutors to deeper insights about justice, courage, and the nature of the soul. This emphasis on introspection and self-awareness laid an important foundation for later psychological thought.

3.8. Plato

Plato (c. 427–347 BCE) built upon Socrates' ideas and created one of the most comprehensive philosophical systems in history. He wrote extensively in the form of dialogues, covering topics like epistemology, metaphysics, ethics, politics, and human psychology. One of his key contributions to the understanding of mind is his concept of the "Forms" (or "Ideas"). Plato believed that the Forms are perfect, eternal realities existing in a realm beyond our physical world. Everything in the physical world is but an imperfect copy of these ideal Forms.

3.8.1. The Allegory of the Cave

Perhaps Plato's most famous illustration is the Allegory of the Cave, found in **The Republic**. In this allegory, prisoners are chained inside a cave, only able to see shadows of objects projected on a wall by a fire behind them. Because they have never seen the actual objects, they mistake the shadows for reality. If a prisoner escapes and sees the real objects (and eventually the sun), he realizes that what he once believed to be real was merely a projection.

Psychologically, this allegory suggests that the mind is trapped by illusions stemming from the senses. True knowledge, or understanding of the Forms, requires intellectual insight beyond mere sensory data. This early distinction between appearance and reality has parallels in psychology's future debates about perception, cognition, and the sources of knowledge.

3.8.2. The Tripartite Soul

Another essential element of Plato's thought is his model of the soul, which he divides into three parts:

1. **Reason (Logistikon):** The rational aspect, concerned with knowledge and discernment of truth.
2. **Spirit (Thumos):** The source of emotions such as courage and anger, giving energy and drive.
3. **Appetite (Epithumia):** The domain of desires and physical cravings, such as hunger, thirst, and sexual urges.

Plato compared these three parts to a charioteer (Reason) trying to control two horses (Spirit and Appetite). The rational part aims for truth and balance, but the spirited and appetitive parts can lead us astray if not guided properly. This metaphor is one of the earliest attempts to describe internal psychological conflict and the need for self-regulation. Later theories of personality, motivation, and emotion would echo aspects of this tripartite structure in various ways.

3.8.3. Immortality and Knowledge

For Plato, the soul pre-exists the body and retains knowledge of the Forms. Learning, therefore, is a process of "recollection," where the soul remembers what it has always known. This idea has significant psychological implications, as it frames learning as an inward process of awakening latent knowledge. While modern psychology does not generally accept innate knowledge in Plato's sense, debates about nativism (inborn abilities) versus empiricism (knowledge from experience) have continued through the centuries.

3.9. Plato's Influence on the Study of Mind

Plato's writings encouraged a philosophical exploration of moral and intellectual virtues, the nature of reality, and the structure of the human psyche. He emphasized rational discourse, introspection, and the pursuit of higher truths. Many subsequent thinkers—both within Greek culture and beyond—used Plato as a point of departure, whether they agreed or disagreed with his emphasis on the world of Forms.

Plato's Academy, the school he founded in Athens, lasted for centuries. It served as a hub of learning, attracting students who would continue debating and refining ideas about the soul, perception, knowledge, and ethics. This environment directly shaped Aristotle, who would become one of the most influential figures in the history of Western thought—particularly in the development of psychology.

3.10. The Seeds of Scientific Thinking in Plato's Dialogues

Although Plato leaned heavily on rational and ideal concepts, some of his dialogues hint at an early scientific attitude. In the **Timaeus**, for instance, Plato offers a cosmological account involving geometric shapes as the building blocks of reality. While this is speculative and partly mystical, it still reflects a desire to explain natural phenomena with systematic, rational principles rather than purely mythic stories.

Moreover, Plato's recognition of the importance of reason as a guiding force for behavior and thought suggests a method of self-examination. By understanding how reason, spirit, and appetite interact, one might improve personal conduct. This is an early forerunner to the notion that one can systematically study and modify behavior, a core tenet of many later psychological theories and therapies.

3.11. Contrasts Among Socrates, Plato, and the Pre-Socratics

Looking back, we see a clear evolution from the Pre-Socratics to Socrates and Plato:

- **Pre-Socratics:** Focused on the nature of the cosmos, investigating fundamental substances and the concept of change. They paved the way for rational inquiry by looking for natural explanations instead of relying solely on myths.
- **Socrates:** Shifted attention to human ethics, self-knowledge, and the examined life. Although not a "psychologist," his probing questions about virtue, knowledge, and personal responsibility set the stage for understanding human behavior and moral psychology.
- **Plato:** Systematized much of this thought into a cohesive philosophical framework, introducing the Theory of Forms and the tripartite soul. He provided a structured view of how the mind might be organized, what knowledge is, and how moral insight can lead to just actions.

This progression demonstrates how ideas about human nature and the mind were slowly crystallizing. Though the term "psychology" did not exist, the essential components of investigating thought, emotion, motivation, and consciousness were emerging in these philosophical debates.

3.12. Criticisms and Alternative Views

Not everyone in ancient Greece agreed with Plato's emphasis on the world of Forms or his model of the soul. Materialists argued that everything, including consciousness, was physical. Skeptics questioned whether we could ever be certain of any knowledge. Nevertheless, Plato's conceptualization of the soul remained influential for centuries, especially when Christian theologians later adopted and adapted many of his ideas into their spiritual frameworks.

Likewise, Socrates' approach, as recorded by Plato, was sometimes criticized for being elusive. He claimed to know nothing while exposing ignorance in others. This method did not always yield a final, definitive answer, leading to frustration among contemporaries who wanted clearer conclusions. Even so, his stress on questioning assumptions and seeking truth through dialogue became a hallmark of Western intellectual culture.

3.13. Education, Politics, and Psychology

Another angle to consider is the link between these philosophical ideas and broader Greek society. Athenian democracy placed a premium on rhetoric, debate, and civic participation. If the mind could be honed to reason clearly, make moral judgments, and debate effectively, a person could rise in public life. The Sophists capitalized on this, teaching rhetoric and argumentation as tools for success. Socrates, meanwhile, believed that moral insight was more important than mere persuasive skill. Plato, disillusioned with Athens' political processes—especially after the execution of Socrates—argued that only philosopher-kings, guided by pure reason, should govern.

Each stance reveals a different perspective on how the mind should be used or cultivated for societal good. These debates about education, politics, and the proper study of human nature fed directly into emerging views on the mind's structure and capabilities. It became clear that how one understands human psychology has practical implications for governance, ethics, and social order.

3.14. Plato's Legacy for Future Psychological Thought

Plato's dialogues tackled subjects like love (**Symposium** and **Phaedrus**), knowledge (**Theaetetus**), the afterlife (**Phaedo**), and the ideal state (**Republic**). Embedded in these works are countless reflections on human motivation, emotion, cognition, and moral development. For instance, in the **Symposium**, different speakers discuss the nature of love and desire, offering insights into affection, lust, and admiration that prefigure later attempts to categorize emotional states.

Although we do not find detailed experiments or scientific proofs in these texts, we do find a systematic approach to questioning and theorizing about human nature. Plato believed that rational thought, if properly cultivated, could guide the baser parts of our nature toward harmonious living. His vision of a soul that transcends mere bodily existence greatly influenced how later Western societies framed discussions about morality, personal growth, and the possibility of divine or eternal aspects to human consciousness.

CHAPTER 4: ARISTOTLE AND HELLENISTIC PSYCHOLOGY

4.1. The Intellectual Milieu After Plato

Plato's Academy remained a center of learning in Athens for centuries, drawing students interested in philosophy, mathematics, astronomy, and more. Among Plato's pupils was Aristotle (384–322 BCE), who studied at the Academy for around twenty years. When Plato died, Aristotle left Athens and eventually founded his own school, the Lyceum.

Aristotle's approach reflected a desire to gather empirical observations about the natural world. He wrote treatises on biology, physics, logic, ethics, politics, and what we can call psychology. While he shared Plato's interest in understanding the soul, he had a different view about how we come to know things. Instead of relying on the recollection of eternal Forms, Aristotle insisted on analyzing and categorizing experiences in the physical world.

As we proceed, we will see how Aristotle's ideas about the mind, sense perception, and cognition formed a significant foundation for later thinkers. After Aristotle, we enter the Hellenistic period, a time marked by the spread of Greek culture across the Mediterranean and the Near East following Alexander the Great's conquests. During this era, new schools of thought, such as Stoicism and Epicureanism, each had their own take on human psychology. Together, Aristotle's systematic approach and the Hellenistic focus on ethics and emotional well-being shaped a substantial part of ancient psychological thought.

4.2. Aristotle's Concept of the Soul (Psyche)

Aristotle discussed the soul in works like *De Anima* (*On the Soul*), where he defined the soul not as a separate spiritual substance but as the "form" of a living body. To Aristotle, a living thing was a unity of matter (the body) and form (the soul). Rather than viewing the soul as something that existed independently in a realm of Forms, he considered it the essence that gives a being its vital functions.

4.2.1. Hierarchy of Souls

Aristotle identified three main types of souls, arranged in a hierarchy from simplest to most complex:

1. **Nutritive Soul**: Found in plants. This soul is responsible for basic functions like growth and reproduction.
2. **Sensitive Soul**: Found in animals. In addition to growth, it allows sensation (sight, hearing, taste, etc.) and some level of locomotion.
3. **Rational Soul**: Unique to humans. This includes the powers of reasoning and intellect.

A human being, in Aristotle's view, contains all three levels of the soul. We can grow, move, sense, and also engage in rational thought. By proposing this structure, Aristotle created a natural continuity between the simplest forms of life and the complexity of human cognition. This hierarchy also laid groundwork for future attempts to link mental capacities to biological structures.

4.2.2. Sense Perception and the Mind

One of Aristotle's significant contributions to early psychology is his analysis of how we perceive the world. He argued that senses pick up "forms" of objects without absorbing their material. For example, when we see a color, the eye receives the "form" of that color. This might sound abstract, but for Aristotle it explained how perception could occur without physical objects literally entering the body.

He also described a concept known as the "common sense," an internal faculty that integrates information from the different senses. This "common sense" was not simply the everyday notion of practical judgment but a specific function that unifies sight, sound, smell, taste, and touch into a coherent perception of the world. Aristotle even speculated about memory and imagination, suggesting that these faculties store and manipulate the forms perceived by the senses.

4.2.3. Intellect: Passive and Active

Aristotle introduced the idea of two types of intellect: the passive intellect and the active intellect. The passive intellect receives and holds the forms derived from sensory experience, while the active intellect is the part that abstracts universal concepts from these forms. The nature of the active intellect is somewhat mysterious in Aristotle's texts; later commentators debated whether it was divine, immortal, or purely a function of the human mind.

Although Aristotle never developed a strict scientific experiment for studying the mind, his careful approach to categorizing faculties like sense perception, memory, imagination, and intellect was a leap forward in systematically describing mental processes. Future philosophers and theologians, especially in the medieval period, would rely heavily on his framework when discussing the nature of the soul.

4.3. Aristotle's Influence on Later Thought

For centuries, Aristotle's works served as a cornerstone of learning in the Mediterranean and Middle East. Translated into Arabic during the Islamic Golden Age, and later into Latin in medieval Europe, his texts provided a structured approach to logic, biology, and what we now call psychology. His emphasis on observation, classification, and rational analysis helped shape early scientific traditions.

Aristotle's stress on the importance of sense perception also fed into debates about empiricism versus rationalism. By placing sense experience at the core of knowledge acquisition, he departed from Plato's more mystical view of recollecting eternal Forms. This difference would echo through later history, influencing how scholars thought about the development of the mind and the role of experience in shaping character and knowledge.

4.4. The Hellenistic Context

After Aristotle, the Greek world underwent massive changes. Alexander the Great spread Greek culture across a vast region, creating a cosmopolitan environment where Greek, Persian, Egyptian, and other traditions mingled. This period, known as the Hellenistic age (roughly 323–31 BCE), saw the rise of major philosophical schools that tackled ethical and psychological questions in ways suited to a world that was no longer confined to the independent city-states of classical Greece.

The Hellenistic schools we will briefly examine—Stoicism, Epicureanism, and Skepticism—each offered distinctive views on how to achieve mental tranquility and a well-ordered life. While we would not call them "psychological schools" in the modern sense, they did present structured ideas about human nature, emotion, motivation, and cognition.

4.5. The Stoics

4.5.1. Founding and Core Beliefs

Stoicism was founded by Zeno of Citium (c. 334–262 BCE). Zeno and his followers held their discussions in the "Stoa Poikile" (Painted Porch) in Athens, hence the name Stoics. One of the central Stoic doctrines was that the cosmos is governed by a rational principle known as the *logos*, and human beings, as rational creatures, should aim to live in accordance with that principle.

The Stoics believed that virtue is the sole good and vice the sole evil. External factors like wealth, status, or even health were considered "indifferent," meaning they do not affect the moral worth of a person. This focus on rational virtue was tied to a disciplined approach toward emotions.

4.5.2. Understanding the Passions

In Stoic psychology, passions (emotions) were viewed as disturbances arising from erroneous judgments. For example, fear occurs when we judge something as an impending evil, and anger happens when we see an offense as worthy of retaliation. Since the Stoics believed that correct reasoning can prevent these wrong judgments, they taught that a wise person remains free from strong passions, achieving a state called *apatheia* (freedom from passion).

While some might see this as suppression of emotion, the Stoics viewed it more as a transformation of emotional life through rational insight. If you can correct the beliefs that cause anxiety or rage, you can keep calm. Although modern therapy techniques are different, there is a distant resemblance between Stoic techniques of reappraising situations and certain cognitive strategies used today.

4.5.3. Stoic Views on Mind and Nature

The Stoics generally held a materialistic view of the soul, believing it to be a physical entity made of subtle matter (often described as a mixture of fire and air). Their reasoning for a material soul aligned with their broader cosmology that everything, including the divine logos, is ultimately corporeal. However, they also believed the soul had distinct parts, such as a ruling faculty located in the chest area. This faculty was responsible for rational thought and moral decision-making.

This emphasis on rational control over emotion would have a long life in Western thought. Later Roman Stoics, like Seneca and Marcus Aurelius, wrote extensively about self-control, moral duty, and the significance of maintaining inner tranquility despite external chaos. Their works would influence Christian ascetic traditions and, in modern times, shape ideas about self-discipline and personal responsibility.

4.6. Epicureanism

4.6.1. Epicurus and His School

Epicurus (341–270 BCE) founded a school in Athens called "The Garden." Epicurean philosophy is often misunderstood as advocating reckless pursuit of pleasure. In reality, Epicurus taught a measured approach, holding that the highest good is the absence of pain (both physical and mental), which leads to a state of tranquility (known as *ataraxia*).

Like Democritus before him, Epicurus was an atomist. He believed that the world, including human beings and their souls, was composed of tiny, indivisible particles. The gods, if they existed, did not interfere in human affairs. Therefore, fear of divine punishment was misplaced and a major source of unnecessary anxiety. By freeing oneself from such fears, one could achieve peace of mind.

4.6.2. The Psychology of Desire and Emotion

Epicurean psychology posited that human action is driven by a desire to seek pleasure and avoid pain. Importantly, Epicurus distinguished between natural and necessary desires (such as food, shelter, friendship) and unnatural or vain desires (such as luxury and fame). Pursuing only the natural and necessary desires leads to a life free from distress, whereas chasing extravagant pleasures can result in frustration, dependence, and mental turmoil.

This emphasis on the correct management of desire has psychological overtones. Epicurus taught that by understanding the nature of desires, we can moderate them, focusing on what is truly necessary for well-being. Like the Stoics, Epicureans aimed to provide a rational framework for living, although they disagreed with the Stoics on many points, particularly about the nature of the divine and the role of fate.

4.6.3. Death and Anxiety

A significant aspect of Epicurean thought is the idea that "death is nothing to us." Since Epicurus believed the soul dissolves upon death (as it is made of atoms), there is no afterlife of torment or reward. This teaching was meant to free people from the fear of death, which Epicurus saw as a primary cause of anxiety. By removing this fear, a person could live more serenely in the present.

In modern terms, Epicureanism offered a kind of therapeutic philosophy. It tried to soothe psychological unrest by rational arguments about the nature of the universe and the soul's mortality. As with Stoicism, this approach demonstrates that ancient philosophy often functioned as a set of psychological techniques, guiding individuals on how to handle fear, longing, and interpersonal relationships.

4.7. Skepticism

4.7.1. Pyrrho and the Skeptics

Another influential Hellenistic movement was Skepticism, associated with thinkers like Pyrrho of Elis (c. 360–270 BCE). Skeptics argued that certain knowledge is either impossible or extremely difficult to attain. As a result, the proper attitude is one of suspension of judgment.

Pyrrho's main goal was to achieve mental peace. He believed that if we stop trying to establish definitive truths about the world, we can avoid the anxiety that comes from dogmatic beliefs. This position had psychological implications. By suspending judgment, a person could remain calm in the face of uncertainty.

4.7.2. Later Skeptics and Psychological Calm

The later Sextus Empiricus (2nd or 3rd century CE) expanded on Pyrrhonism. In his works, he discussed how skeptics used specific arguments to show the relativity of perceptions and the contradictions in dogmatic philosophies. While Skepticism does not propose a "theory of the mind" in a systematic way, it does address mental states. It presents the idea that freedom from disturbance (*ataraxia*) results from not clinging to any absolute position.

In an age of many competing philosophical systems, Skepticism offered a mental strategy: recognize that different cultures and schools see the world differently, and that no single explanation can be proven with certainty. This perspective can reduce inner conflict, since one is not bound to defend a rigid set of dogmas. Thus, Skepticism's psychological contribution lay in its method of dealing with doubt and uncertainty.

4.8. The Common Thread

Though Stoics, Epicureans, and Skeptics disagreed on metaphysics and epistemology, they shared a major interest in achieving a state of tranquility or well-being—often referred to by the Greek word *eudaimonia*, which can be translated as "flourishing" or "good spirit." Each school offered methods to handle emotions, desires, and beliefs in a way that would foster mental harmony:

- **Stoicism**: Control passions through rational judgment.
- **Epicureanism**: Manage desires and overcome fear (especially fear of death).
- **Skepticism**: Suspend judgment to avoid distress from dogmatic disputes.

In this Hellenistic tradition, we see a more explicit emphasis on "therapies" for the mind, even though they were philosophical in nature. Philosophical schools functioned somewhat like modern counseling or therapy groups, guiding individuals toward coping strategies for life's difficulties.

4.9. Differences from Earlier Greek Thought

Compared to Plato and Aristotle, who devoted significant attention to metaphysical structures and systematic analyses of knowledge, the Hellenistic schools focused more on practical ethics and psychological well-being. While Plato aimed to discover eternal truths about the Forms, and Aristotle sought to categorize nature systematically, the Stoics, Epicureans, and Skeptics asked, "How can we be at peace in a turbulent world?" Their answers were not just theoretical; they provided daily practices, exercises in mindfulness, and techniques for calming the mind.

This shift was partly due to the changing social and political environment. With the decline of independent city-states and the rise of large empires, people felt less in control of their political destiny. So personal serenity and moral self-management took on greater importance. This focus on inner life foreshadowed future philosophical and religious movements that emphasized personal salvation, spiritual peace, or enlightenment—elements that also intersect with psychological concerns about stress, anxiety, and emotional balance.

4.10. Legacy of Aristotle and Hellenistic Psychology

The ideas from this era deeply influenced later intellectual traditions in the Roman period, early Christian thought, and eventually the Islamic Golden Age. Aristotle's works, in particular, became foundational texts. Hellenistic philosophies, especially Stoicism, appealed to Roman elites like Seneca and Marcus Aurelius, who adapted Greek ideas into Latin works that continued to shape ethical thought for centuries.

When Christianity began to spread, Church Fathers wrestled with Greek philosophical heritage. They debated which ideas about the soul, virtue, and reason could be integrated into Christian doctrine. Aristotelian philosophy, with its systematic approach, became especially important in the medieval period, influencing scholars such as Thomas Aquinas. Stoic notions of self-control and universal reason also resonated with aspects of Christian morality.

In these transitions, we see how concepts of the mind—reason, emotion, the soul—did not remain static but were adapted to new cultural and religious contexts. This adaptability is part of what makes the history of psychology so rich: older philosophical frameworks often re-emerged in fresh forms, each time impacting the way people explained and managed mental life.

CHAPTER 5: THE ROMAN ERA AND EARLY CHRISTIAN INFLUENCES

5.1. Introduction to the Roman Context

By the time Rome rose to dominate the Mediterranean world, Greek philosophy and science had already established deep roots. Greek cultural influence did not vanish with Rome's ascendancy; rather, Greek ideas blended into Roman life. The Romans admired the intellectual heritage of the Greeks. Wealthy Roman citizens often hired Greek tutors to educate their children in literature, rhetoric, and philosophy. This cultural exchange had a direct impact on how Romans discussed and understood the mind, behavior, and morality.

But Rome added its own layer. Roman society placed a high value on practical affairs—law, administration, and social order. This pragmatism merged with Greek intellectual traditions, resulting in philosophical outlooks that were concerned not only with theoretical questions but also with day-to-day conduct and governance. Many Roman philosophers, such as Cicero, Seneca, Epictetus, and Marcus Aurelius, were actually steeped in Greek thought, especially Stoicism. Meanwhile, developments in Roman medicine—particularly through Galen—shaped early understandings of both the body and the mind.

Over time, Christianity emerged as a major force in the Roman Empire. Early Christian thinkers, including Tertullian, Origen, and later Augustine, integrated Greek philosophy with Christian doctrine. This fusion led to new views of the soul, sin, free will, and human purpose. The shift from a pagan empire to a Christian one profoundly affected how people interpreted mental states and moral responsibilities. By examining these dynamics, we see how Roman practicality, Greek philosophy, and Christian theology converged to form a distinct chapter in the story of psychology's early history.

5.2. Roman Adaptations of Greek Philosophy

5.2.1. Popularity of Stoicism in Rome

Stoicism, which we introduced in the previous chapter, found a receptive audience in Rome. There were good reasons for this. The Roman Empire was vast, and individuals often felt a sense of powerlessness in the face of wars, political strife, or personal misfortunes. Stoic teachings on emotional control, virtue, and acceptance of fate resonated with people who needed inner stability amid external chaos.

- **Cicero (106-43 BCE)**: Although he was not a Stoic himself—he moved among various philosophical schools—Cicero played a huge role in introducing Greek philosophy to Latin readers. In works like *Tusculan Disputations* and *On the Ends of Good and Evil*, he discussed morality, the nature of the gods, and the role of the mind in achieving a good life. Cicero highlighted the idea that philosophy is a practical guide for living, not just abstract speculation.
- **Seneca (c. 4 BCE-65 CE)**: A statesman and philosopher, Seneca embraced Stoicism more fully. In his letters and essays, he examined anger, fear, love, and other emotions, offering practical advice on how to manage them through reason. Seneca believed that while emotions arise naturally, we can control how we respond to them by adjusting our judgments. This approach emphasized that the mind's interpretation of

events is key to our emotional states, aligning closely with core Stoic principles.
- **Epictetus (c. 50–135 CE)**: Born a slave, Epictetus later gained freedom and taught Stoic philosophy. His recorded teachings (in the *Discourses* and the *Enchiridion*) argue that our true power lies in how we perceive and react to external events, not in controlling those events themselves. Epictetus stressed the concept of "what is in our power" (our attitudes and choices) versus "what is not in our power" (external circumstances). This distinction laid the groundwork for a psychologically astute approach, highlighting internal locus of control as a pathway to tranquility.
- **Marcus Aurelius (121–180 CE)**: The Roman Emperor wrote *Meditations* as a personal journal, reflecting daily on Stoic ideas. He analyzed his own thoughts and motivations, examining how he might align with universal reason (*logos*) despite the burdens of leading a vast empire. Marcus Aurelius's introspective style offers a glimpse of a leader applying a philosophical method as a form of self-regulation.

In these Roman Stoics, we see a strong focus on coping mechanisms for stress and adversity—methods that resemble a basic psychological therapy. Their writings address how to cultivate an internal state of calm, how to reframe adverse events, and how to practice self-discipline. These concepts would echo in later centuries when thinkers sought guidance on moral and mental well-being.

5.2.2. Eclectic Philosophical Approaches

Not every Roman intellectual was a strict Stoic. Some, like Cicero, took an eclectic stance, drawing from multiple Greek schools—Academic Skepticism, Stoicism, Epicureanism—to form a pragmatic philosophy suited to Roman needs. This eclecticism underscores the Roman attitude: if a doctrine or technique was useful in daily life, it deserved attention.

One effect of this eclecticism was a fluid exchange of ideas regarding the human mind and emotions. Romans frequently debated what role divine powers played in mental processes, whether virtue was enough to secure happiness, and how to cultivate resilience. Their discussions broadened the conversation about inner life, ensuring that the psychological dimension of philosophy remained alive.

5.2.3. The Role of Rhetoric and Oratory

Roman society placed a premium on oratory skills for political and legal endeavors. Training in rhetoric often touched on psychological concepts, because persuading an audience requires understanding human emotions, beliefs, and motivations. Teachers of rhetoric taught budding politicians and lawyers how to sway crowds by appealing to sympathy, fear, hope, or moral duty. In doing so, they delved into how language shapes thought and feeling—an early glimpse of a "social psychology" element.

Though not formal experimental science, Roman rhetorical handbooks recognized that people respond to emotional triggers and well-crafted arguments. This knowledge highlighted the mind's malleability and the importance of perception in shaping judgment. Hence, even in the realm of public speaking, we see an implicit psychology: understanding how to move or calm the passions of an audience.

5.3. Roman Medicine and the Mind

5.3.1. Galen's Background and Influence

A major figure connecting Roman thought to the history of psychology is **Galen** (129–c. 216 CE). Born in Pergamum (in modern-day Turkey), Galen studied medicine extensively before working as a physician in Rome, eventually serving several emperors. His medical writings dominated Western medical theory for over a millennium and influenced Middle Eastern scholars during the Islamic Golden Age.

While primarily known as a physician, Galen's work touched on what we would now call "psychological" issues. He built upon Hippocrates's four-humor theory—blood, phlegm, yellow bile, and black bile—linking these humors to temperament and personality. He reasoned that each individual's mental and emotional life was partly determined by the balance of these bodily fluids.

5.3.2. The Four Temperaments

Expanding on Hippocrates, Galen posited that people exhibit one of four basic temperaments, each associated with one humor:

1. **Sanguine** (blood): Characterized by cheerfulness, optimism, and a lively nature.
2. **Phlegmatic** (phlegm): Marked by calmness, slowness, and a less emotional demeanor.
3. **Choleric** (yellow bile): Identified with anger, energy, and ambition.
4. **Melancholic** (black bile): Associated with sadness, introspection, and sometimes depression.

Though this theory is outdated by modern standards, it represented a systematic attempt to explain personality differences through physiological processes. Galen also believed that imbalances in humors contributed to mental disturbances. For example, excess black bile could trigger melancholic moods, while too much yellow bile might lead to aggression or irritability.

5.3.3. Mind-Body Relationship in Galen's Work

Galen leaned toward a monistic view of the human being, seeing the mind and body as closely linked. He located certain mental functions in the brain, following earlier anatomical work by physicians like

Herophilus and Erasistratus. However, Galen's primary explanation for personality and mood still centered on the fluid-humor model.

Galen's influence on later psychology is indirect but substantial. Because his medical writings became authoritative for centuries, many scholars adopted his physiological approach to mental issues, focusing on bodily balances and imbalances as explanations for temperament. Even in the Middle Ages, the humoral theory was used to interpret and treat what we would now call mental illnesses or mood disorders.

5.4. Transition to Early Christian Influences

5.4.1. The Spread of Christianity

Christianity began as a small Jewish sect in the eastern Mediterranean, slowly spreading westward through missionary work and trade routes. Over the first three centuries CE, Christians faced periods of persecution but also gained converts across social classes. Emperor Constantine's conversion in the early 4th century dramatically changed the faith's status, leading to eventual dominance throughout the empire.

This shift altered cultural conversations about the soul, morality, and the nature of divine grace. While Greek and Roman philosophies had approached such topics from a rational or natural perspective, Christianity introduced new concepts: original sin, salvation, and an afterlife with heaven or hell. Over time, Christian thinkers adapted elements of Greek philosophy, merging them with scriptural teachings to form a Christian intellectual tradition.

5.4.2. Tertullian, Origen, and the Early Christian Mind

Early Christian authors, such as Tertullian (c. 155–220 CE) in North Africa and Origen (c. 184–253 CE) in Alexandria, contributed to shaping how believers thought about the mind and soul. Tertullian argued that the soul was a real, material entity "stamped" with divine knowledge of God, though he also stressed the importance of faith over purely rational speculation. Origen, on the other hand, drew from Platonic ideas, proposing that souls pre-existed their earthly lives. Both wrote treatises that engaged with philosophical themes inherited from Greek tradition, but they did so through a lens of Christian doctrine.

Christianity emphasized human free will, personal accountability, and the potential for spiritual transformation. These concepts, when combined with existing Greek thoughts on reason and virtue, led to new ideas about human psychology. For instance, sin became linked not just to external acts but to inner thoughts and desires. Thus, introspection gained spiritual weight, as believers were urged to examine their consciences for hidden faults.

5.5. Augustine of Hippo

No figure was more significant in shaping early Christian views of the mind than **Augustine of Hippo (354–430 CE)**. Augustine's intellectual journey began with exposure to various philosophies, including Manichaeism, Neo-Platonism, and Stoicism, before he converted to Christianity. In his writings—most famously *Confessions*, *On the Trinity*, and *The City of God*—Augustine laid out a comprehensive vision of the soul, free will, memory, and divine grace.

5.5.1. Augustine's Concept of the Soul and Memory

Augustine's *Confessions* is notable for its introspective style. He used personal reflection to examine his own thoughts, motivations, and sins. This deep self-analysis was a breakthrough in Western literature, emphasizing the mind's interior life as a subject worthy of extensive scrutiny. Unlike many earlier philosophers, Augustine's approach was not purely theoretical. It was personal, emotional, and spiritual.

In *Confessions*, Augustine explores memory in a way that foreshadows later psychological curiosity. He considered memory a vast storehouse of images and experiences, some conscious and some forgotten until triggered. He used the metaphor of an immense inner space containing recollections of the senses, learned knowledge, and emotional experiences. This notion that memory could store layers of experiences influenced subsequent medieval writers and helped lay a foundation for analyzing how the mind organizes and retrieves information.

5.5.2. Will, Sin, and Divine Grace

Augustine also wrote extensively on the concept of the will (*voluntas*). He believed that the will is central to moral action and that human beings are free moral agents—but that this freedom is wounded by original sin. From a psychological perspective, Augustine is arguing that the mind is not a blank slate of rational capacities; it is also shaped by an inherited inclination to wrongdoing. Hence, an internal struggle ensues between what we should do and what we desire to do.

He introduced the idea that divine grace is necessary for the will to overcome sinful urges. While earlier philosophers, especially the Stoics, emphasized self-discipline as the route to virtue, Augustine stressed that humans cannot fully control their own minds without God's help. This theological perspective changed the conversation about mental processes: virtues and vices were not solely a matter of rational choices but also of spiritual influence and divine intervention.

5.5.3. Neo-Platonic Influences on Augustine

Neo-Platonism, a philosophical system developed by Plotinus (204–270 CE) and others, deeply influenced Augustine. Neo-Platonists taught that ultimate reality is the One, from which the soul can ascend by turning away from the material world. Augustine adapted these ideas, identifying the One with the Christian God. Thus, the soul's journey is not simply an ascent through philosophical contemplation but also a journey of faith toward divine unity.

This Neo-Platonic model reinforced Augustine's view that the soul is meant to orient itself toward God, away from earthly distractions. It also bolstered the idea that spiritual truths can be discovered through internal reflection and prayer. This approach to the mind—introspective, reliant on inner vision—would become a hallmark of medieval Christian thought on psychology and spirituality.

5.6. The Merging of Roman Pragmatism and Christian Ideals

By Augustine's time, the Western Roman Empire was under significant pressure from internal strife and invasions. The older Roman virtues of discipline and civic duty now mixed with Christian teachings about charity, humility, and salvation. This cultural blend affected how people thought about mental life:

- **Moral Responsibility**: Romans prized personal responsibility, a viewpoint the Christians now reframed in terms of sin, repentance, and divine judgment.
- **Public versus Private**: Roman political life emphasized public service, but Christian spirituality emphasized internal purity of heart and soul. This new internal focus gave rise to more

elaborate discussions of mental states—temptation, guilt, contrition—that might not be visible externally.
- **Introspection**: Roman Stoicism had taught self-examination, but Christianity added the dimension of confession and atonement, making introspection a regular practice for believers.

These factors combined to produce a culture where the "psychological" dimension of religion—feelings of remorse, states of grace, spiritual anguish—became a central topic. Augustine's writings, along with other Church Fathers, anchored these issues in a theological framework that would dominate the medieval period.

5.7. The Later Roman Empire and Beyond

5.7.1. Monastic Traditions

As the Roman Empire transformed, monastic communities began to form. These communities placed emphasis on prayer, meditation, and scriptural study. Early monks and nuns practiced various forms of asceticism, fasting, and isolation, which in turn provided experiences that might be called "extreme psychological states." Within monasteries, spiritual directors guided novices through struggles with doubt, anxiety, and temptation, effectively acting as early "counselors" for spiritual-mental welfare.

Though these practices were religious, they had psychological elements. The advice given by experienced monks often resembled a kind of therapy, instructing the less experienced on how to handle intrusive thoughts or maintain focus in prayer. Over time, monastic traditions developed subtle understandings of how solitude, community life, and spiritual exercises affect the mind.

5.7.2. Cassian and the Eight Vices

John Cassian (c. 360–435 CE), an influential monk, wrote about eight principal vices that disturb the mind—gluttony, lust, greed, anger, etc. He and other desert fathers classified these as mental or spiritual ailments requiring remedies like humility, prayer, vigilance, and confession. Though couched in religious language, such classifications show an early attempt to categorize harmful mental patterns and devise systematic solutions.

These desert fathers' reflections would feed into the later Christian tradition of identifying and treating the "passions" or "vices." This was not quite psychological science, but it was a framework for understanding how certain recurring mental habits could lead to distress or sin and how spiritual discipline could reorient the mind toward virtue.

5.7.3. Decline of the Western Empire, Rise of the Eastern Empire

In the 5th century CE, the Western Roman Empire declined due to various pressures—economic, military, and political. However, the Eastern Roman (Byzantine) Empire continued for nearly a thousand years more. Byzantine culture preserved many Greek texts, including works by Aristotle, Galen, and others, while also developing Eastern Christian theology. This meant that the Greek philosophical heritage remained alive in the East, influencing Christian thought and eventually contributing to the preservation of philosophical and medical knowledge that would later re-enter Western Europe.

5.8. Impact on Subsequent Eras

The Roman era, capped by the rise of Christianity, sowed seeds for much of the medieval framework of psychology. Major legacies include:

1. **Integration of Moral Philosophy and Daily Life**: Roman Stoicism and other schools showed how philosophical reflection can guide personal conduct.
2. **Physiological Perspective**: Galen's humoral theory remained the dominant medical model, linking bodily fluids to personality and mood.
3. **Christian Introspection**: Early Christian teachings and figures like Augustine placed heightened importance on the inner life—memory, will, guilt, and divine grace. This set the stage for the Middle Ages, where theology would deeply shape conceptions of the mind.
4. **Preservation and Adaptation**: Byzantine scholars and early medieval monastic communities safeguarded Greek and Roman writings, allowing for their eventual rediscovery in the West.

CHAPTER 6: THE MIDDLE AGES IN EUROPE

6.1. Framing the Medieval Period

The Middle Ages in Europe, usually dated from the 5th to the late 15th century, covers nearly a thousand years. This era began with the fall of the Western Roman Empire and ended on the cusp of the Renaissance. During this long span, Europe saw dramatic changes: new kingdoms formed, Islam arose and spread, and interactions between the Christian West and the Islamic world changed the flow of knowledge. Monasteries and cathedrals emerged as centers of learning. Universities eventually took shape, providing institutional frameworks where philosophical and theological questions were debated.

Understanding the human mind in the Middle Ages was deeply tied to religious beliefs. The Catholic Church dominated intellectual life in Western Europe. Scholars considered themselves theologians first, philosophers second. Almost every discussion about human nature and mental processes was filtered through Christian doctrines. Yet these discussions also absorbed ancient Greek ideas, especially the works of Aristotle, which re-entered Western Europe mainly through Arabic translations. This mix, known as Scholasticism, became the hallmark of medieval intellectual culture.

6.2. The Early Medieval Period: Preserving Knowledge

6.2.1. Monastic Learning and Scriptoria

After the fall of the Western Roman Empire, continuous warfare and political fragmentation made travel and trade difficult. The once-thriving urban culture of the Mediterranean declined, and many of the libraries and centers of learning that had existed under Roman rule disappeared or fell into disuse. Meanwhile, literacy in the Latin West declined sharply among the general population. However, monasteries provided a new haven for literacy.

Monks painstakingly copied manuscripts in *scriptoria*, preserving works by Church Fathers and some classical authors. While Greek language skills became rare in the West, certain essential texts in Latin (like some of Augustine's writings) survived. This stage was less about developing new theories of the mind and more about preventing complete intellectual collapse. The idea of mental and moral guidance persisted through religious practices—confession, ascetic discipline, and spiritual contemplation—rather than systematic philosophical discourse.

6.2.2. Influence of Augustine and the Desert Fathers

The writings of Augustine, introduced in the previous chapter, played a major role in shaping medieval views of the mind. His introspective approach and emphasis on grace and sin resonated deeply in monastic culture. Monks read Augustine's *Confessions* and other works to guide their spiritual journeys, focusing on humility, obedience, and the constant scrutiny of one's internal thoughts.

In addition, the spiritual practices from Eastern Christian monasticism (the "desert fathers") also influenced Western monks. Texts describing how to handle "passions" or "vices" were adapted into Latin guides. These described methods for overcoming temptations like anger, sloth, and lust through prayer, fasting, and self-awareness. Although couched in theological language, these guides often offered keen observations on human desires and the difficulties of controlling one's own mind.

6.2.3. Boethius and the Bridge to Scholasticism

One figure who kept the light of classical thought alive was **Boethius (c. 477–524 CE)**. He translated some of Aristotle's works from Greek to Latin and wrote *The Consolation of Philosophy*, a philosophical treatise that blended Christian and Platonic ideas. While Boethius's direct impact on medieval psychology was limited, his writings formed a key link between the classical world and the emerging medieval intellectual climate. He exemplified the possibility of integrating Christian faith with Greek philosophical reasoning—a theme that would define the Scholastic period.

6.3. The High Middle Ages

6.3.1. Establishment of Universities

Around the 12th century, Europe saw the rise of the first universities, including those in Bologna, Paris, and Oxford. These institutions were initially focused on training clergy and lawyers, but they gradually expanded to include the study of "liberal arts" (grammar, rhetoric, logic, arithmetic, geometry, music, and astronomy) and higher disciplines like theology, medicine, and law. Logic (or dialectic) was central, reflecting a method of inquiry based on structured debate and reference to authoritative texts—particularly Scripture and the Church Fathers.

Scholasticism emerged in this environment as a method that combined rigorous logical argumentation with Christian doctrinal commitments. Scholars engaged with philosophical texts—especially Aristotle—through a process of commentary, question, and disputation. The aim was to reconcile apparent contradictions, including reconciling Aristotle's naturalism with Christian theology. This reconciliation often involved discussing the human soul: its origin, powers, and destiny.

6.3.2. Rediscovery of Aristotle

Aristotle's works had never been entirely lost in the Eastern Roman (Byzantine) Empire. But in the Latin West, only a few of his logical writings were known during the early Middle Ages. Translations from Arabic sources (especially in Spain and Sicily) reintroduced Europe to Aristotle's full corpus in the 12th and 13th centuries. Along with Aristotle came the commentaries of great Islamic scholars like Avicenna (Ibn Sina) and Averroes (Ibn Rushd), who had their own interpretations of the soul and intellect.

This influx of knowledge triggered debates, as Aristotle's perspective sometimes appeared to conflict with Christian doctrine—most notably on issues like the eternity of the world and the nature of the individual soul after death. Yet Scholastics eagerly embraced Aristotle's framework for categorizing the faculties of the soul (e.g., vegetative, sensitive, rational). They found it helpful for systematic theology and for describing how humans perceive, reason, and will.

6.3.3. Peter Abelard and Early Scholastic Method

Before Thomas Aquinas rose to prominence, thinkers like **Peter Abelard (1079–1142)** exemplified the early Scholastic approach. Abelard's *Sic et Non* (Yes and No) collected apparently contradictory statements from Church authorities, then challenged students to resolve them using logical tools. This method underscored the importance of reasoned argument and textual analysis as a pathway to truth.

Abelard also discussed ethics and the mind, particularly focusing on intentions and conscience. He believed moral responsibility hinged on what a person intended, not only on the external act. This implied a deeper concern for a person's internal state—thoughts, motivations—another instance of how Scholastic thinkers dealt with psychological questions in a moral-theological framework.

6.4. Thomas Aquinas

6.4.1. The Life and Context of Aquinas

Thomas Aquinas (1225–1274), a Dominican friar, became the most prominent figure in Scholasticism. Educated in Naples, Cologne, and Paris, he studied under Albertus Magnus (Albert the Great), who was one of the earliest champions of the newly recovered Aristotelian texts. Aquinas aimed to create a comprehensive synthesis of Christian theology and Aristotelian philosophy, culminating in works like the *Summa Theologica* and *Summa Contra Gentiles*.

By Aquinas's time, debate raged over whether Aristotle's naturalistic approach threatened Christian beliefs about the soul's immortality and creation. Some church leaders even banned certain Aristotelian ideas. Aquinas boldly argued that faith and reason, revelation and philosophy, need not conflict but can complement each other.

6.4.2. Aquinas's Faculty Psychology

In line with Aristotle, Aquinas identified different faculties within the soul. However, he gave them a Christian interpretation:

1. **Vegetative (Nutritive)**: The basic life functions—growth, nutrition, reproduction.
2. **Sensitive**: Common to animals and humans, includes sense perception and appetite (sensitive appetites like pleasure and avoidance of pain).

3. **Rational (Intellective)**: Unique to humans, enabling abstract thought, reasoning, and moral choice.

Aquinas distinguished further between the **active intellect** (the power to abstract universal ideas from sense data) and the **passive intellect** (the capacity to be informed by these ideas). He insisted that the soul is the form of the body, echoing Aristotle, but emphasized that each soul is individually created by God and immortal. This resolved some concerns about whether a purely Aristotelian approach might conflict with Christian teachings on personal salvation.

6.4.3. The Will and Moral Psychology

Aquinas devoted significant attention to the will, describing it as a rational appetite oriented toward the good. He explained that when the intellect presents something as good, the will moves toward it. However, this does not eliminate free choice, because the will can choose between different goods, and the intellect can judge them in various ways. This interplay of reason and will shaped medieval moral psychology: sin occurs when the will chooses an apparent good that is lesser than a truly higher good, often due to a clouded or misguided intellect.

Aquinas also tackled the passions, seeing them as neither wholly evil nor automatically virtuous. Instead, passions (like love, hate, joy, sadness, fear) become morally significant depending on how reason guides them. This nuanced view mirrored the Stoic emphasis on rational control of emotion, but Aquinas did not demand the elimination of passions. He argued that well-ordered passions can support virtuous action.

6.5. Other Notable Scholastics and Their Contributions

6.5.1. Duns Scotus

John Duns Scotus (c. 1266–1308) was another important Scholastic who debated Aquinas's views on the will and intellect. Scotus put strong emphasis on the will's independence. Where Aquinas suggested the will follows what the intellect presents as good, Scotus believed the will retained a greater autonomy, which implied a stronger sense of free will. From a psychological perspective, Scotus advanced the discussion on how human beings choose among different possibilities, maintaining that the will can override purely rational calculations.

6.5.2. William of Ockham

William of Ockham (c. 1287–1347) is famous for "Ockham's Razor," the principle that one should not multiply entities beyond necessity. In his philosophical work, Ockham took a more nominalist approach, arguing that universals are simply names (or mental concepts), not real entities existing independently. This viewpoint influenced theories of knowledge, as it challenged the idea that the mind has direct access to universal forms in an external realm. Ockham's perspective placed the source of universals within the mind's own activity, sparking debates on how perception and cognition truly operate.

Though not a psychologist in the modern sense, Ockham's emphasis on simplicity and mental constructs shaped future notions of how humans think and label experiences. His nominalism suggested that much of what we consider "common nature" is a product of the mind's categorizing function, not a pre-existing reality in the external world.

6.6. Medieval Debates on Mind-Body Relationships

6.6.1. Duality and Unity

Medieval thinkers generally followed Aristotle's idea that the soul is the form of the body. Yet a tension remained between the biblical teaching that the soul survives death and the Aristotelian emphasis on the soul-body unity. The standard solution was to say that God miraculously preserves the rational soul after bodily death, eventually reuniting it with a resurrected body at the end of time. This theological stance influenced how scholars talked about "psychology"—they viewed the mind as deeply tied to bodily processes but also capable of existing without the body by divine action.

6.6.2. Sin, Grace, and Psychological States

Medieval theology also insisted that psychological states cannot be fully understood apart from the concepts of sin and grace. When a person experiences anger or despair, medieval theologians might interpret this through the lens of moral failing (sin) or as a temptation that must be overcome with divine help. Confession, penance, and prayer were spiritual "treatments" for mental and moral distress.

While not empirical science, this approach did involve close observation of thoughts, emotions, and motivations—especially among monks, nuns, and priests who guided the faithful. In many ways, these religious practices prefigured some aspects of counseling, focusing on changing one's inner perspective to align with virtue and spiritual well-being.

6.7. Medieval Medicine and the Mind

6.7.1. Continuation of Humoral Theory

Despite the dominance of theology, medieval Europe also continued and adapted the medical theories of Galen. The four humors persisted as the main explanation for diseases, both physical and mental. Doctors would "treat" mental disturbances by balancing humors, employing techniques like bloodletting, diet changes, and herbal remedies.

Physicians such as Constantine the African (11th century) and later medical scholars combined Galenic methods with Arabic medical knowledge, which included new commentaries on mental afflictions. Thus, a nascent "psychological medicine" existed within the humoral framework, though it was not distinct from general medicine.

6.7.2. Hospitals and Care

In the later Middle Ages, the concept of hospitals emerged, often run by religious orders. These institutions provided care for the sick, the poor, and the mentally distressed. While treatment was rudimentary by modern standards, the idea that one could house and care for individuals with mental problems marked a shift from earlier periods, when such people might be left to fend for themselves or subjected to harsh measures. Care might still be a mix of spiritual guidance, prayer, and attempts to restore humor balance, but at least it recognized that mental and physical illnesses needed some form of dedicated attention.

6.8. Women Mystics and Psychological Insight

Though much of medieval intellectual life was male-dominated, women mystics like **Hildegard of Bingen (1098–1179)**, **Julian of**

Norwich (1343–after 1416), and others provided unique insight into the inner life. They recorded visions and spiritual experiences that included intense emotional states, inner dialogues with the divine, and reflections on their sense of self.

For instance, Hildegard of Bingen wrote extensively on health, herbal remedies, and spiritual counsel, blending medical knowledge with mystical insight. Julian of Norwich's *Revelations of Divine Love* delved into the nature of sin, suffering, and divine compassion, offering reflections on how the mind can reconcile pain with faith. Although these works were primarily spiritual, they showed that medieval discussions of the mind were not confined to academic Scholastics but extended into broader religious life, touching on personal experiences of fear, joy, and transcendence.

6.9. The Late Middle Ages and Shifting Mindsets

6.9.1. Scholastic Decline and New Currents

By the 14th century, Scholasticism began to face challenges. Nominalism, exemplified by Ockham, and various theological disputes undercut the once-dominant confidence in the harmonious blending of faith and Aristotelian reason. The Black Death (mid-14th century) also shattered social structures and caused widespread questioning of religious and philosophical certainties. Political upheavals, the Avignon Papacy, and the Great Schism further eroded the Church's moral authority.

In intellectual terms, people started exploring more direct forms of religious expression, such as lay piety movements, and turned to classical sources in a new way during what became the early Renaissance. This included a revived interest in human values, personal experience, and the study of nature for its own sake—foreshadowing the changes we will see in the next era.

6.9.2. Forerunners of Renaissance Humanism

Some late medieval scholars, like Petrarch (1304-1374), criticized the complex disputations of the Scholastics and called for a return to classical literature, not just Aristotle but also Cicero and others, to discover more about the human condition. This attitude laid the foundation for Renaissance Humanism, which would emphasize the dignity and agency of individuals. These developments hinted that new ways of talking about mind and behavior—less tied to rigid theological frameworks—were on the horizon.

6.10. Summary of Medieval Psychology

During the Middle Ages in Europe:

1. **Dominant Role of Theology**: Discussions of the mind were almost always integrated with Christian beliefs about the soul, sin, virtue, and salvation.
2. **Aristotelian Influence**: Scholars used Aristotle's categories to analyze mental faculties, but adapted them to fit Christian doctrine on immortality and divine creation.
3. **Moral Psychology**: Much attention focused on the will, passions, and moral behavior—how reason should guide emotions to live a virtuous life.
4. **Preservation of Classical Knowledge**: Monasteries and later universities carried on Greek and Roman texts, ensuring key ideas about the mind did not vanish.
5. **Medical Views**: Galen's humoral theory continued to dominate understandings of mental disturbances, shaping rudimentary mental healthcare approaches.
6. **Spiritual and Mystical Experiences**: Monastic practices, confessions, and the writings of mystics provided an experiential dimension, emphasizing introspection and inner transformation.

6.11. Transition to the Renaissance

As the medieval period drew to a close, Europe was poised for a cultural revival. The Renaissance would bring renewed interest in classical languages, arts, and direct observation of nature. Humanist scholars would champion the study of individual potential, secular ethics, and beauty—expanding discussions about the mind beyond strictly theological boundaries. Simultaneously, the Islamic Golden Age played a key role in preserving and enhancing Greek texts, fueling cross-cultural exchanges that would fertilize European thought further.

Our story thus moves forward to an age where human-centered thinking gradually replaced the medieval theological framework, setting the stage for the scientific investigations of later centuries. But first, in the next installment, we will turn our gaze to the contributions of Islamic scholars during their own "Golden Age," which overlapped with the European medieval period. There, we will see how philosophers and physicians in the Islamic world preserved Greek heritage and produced new insights on the nature of the mind and the body—insights that would eventually flow back into Europe and reshape Western intellectual life.

CHAPTER 7: THE ISLAMIC GOLDEN AGE

7.1. Introduction

Between the 8th and the 14th centuries, much of the Islamic world experienced a period of remarkable intellectual activity often called the "Islamic Golden Age." This era featured extensive translation movements, significant original research in fields like mathematics and medicine, and philosophical endeavors that combined Greek traditions with Islamic theology. The results of this cultural flourishing impacted many areas of knowledge, including early studies relevant to psychology.

While Western Europe grappled with the aftermath of the Roman Empire's collapse and slowly developed Scholasticism, the Islamic empires—particularly under the Abbasid Caliphate centered in Baghdad—became havens for scholarship. Muslim thinkers eagerly sought out texts from ancient Greece, Persia, and India. They translated Aristotle, Plato, Galen, and others into Arabic, preserving works that might otherwise have been lost. More than preservation, these scholars critiqued, refined, and added their own insights, shaping ideas on the soul, human behavior, and rational thought.

In this chapter, we will trace how Islamic scholars built upon the Greek heritage, what new concepts about the mind they introduced, and how their work later found its way back into Europe, ultimately influencing the Renaissance and beyond. We will also see how religion and philosophy interacted in the Islamic context to produce distinctive ideas about human nature, the workings of the mind, and methods for treating mental disturbances.

7.2. The Translation Movement and the House of Wisdom

7.2.1. Early Efforts

After the Islamic conquests in the 7th century, the new rulers found themselves in territories that had been part of the Byzantine or Persian Empires, where Greek and other scholarly traditions flourished. The Umayyad and later Abbasid Caliphates recognized the value of scientific and philosophical knowledge. Over time, leaders and wealthy patrons sponsored systematic translations of key works from Greek, Syriac, and other languages into Arabic.

These efforts reached a pinnacle under the Abbasids. Caliph Al-Mansur (r. 754–775) is credited with founding Baghdad, which rapidly became an intellectual nexus. A few decades later, under Caliph Harun al-Rashid (r. 786–809) and his son Al-Ma'mun (r. 813–833), a more formal institution—the **Bayt al-Hikmah** or "House of Wisdom"—emerged. In this facility, scholars gathered to translate texts on philosophy, medicine, astronomy, and mathematics.

7.2.2. Importance for Psychology

Within these translations, works by Aristotle and Galen stood out. Aristotle's treatises on the soul (*De Anima*) and logic gained fresh audiences among Arabic-speaking intellectuals. Galen's medical writings, including discussions on temperament and the four humors, also found new life in this context. These texts laid theoretical foundations for thinking about the mind, emotion, and behavior.

Crucially, the scholars did not treat these translations as static truths. They wrote extensive commentaries, critiqued perceived contradictions, and integrated what they found useful into their own philosophical or theological frameworks. The House of Wisdom and similar institutions fostered debate and creative synthesis, which led to original contributions by Muslim philosophers and scientists—often called **falasifa** in the Arabic tradition.

7.3. Notable Figures and Their Contributions

7.3.1. Al-Kindi: The First Arab Philosopher

Al-Kindi (c. 801–873) is often considered the first major Islamic philosopher who tried to reconcile Greek thought with Islamic teachings. He wrote on various subjects, including metaphysics, ethics, and, importantly, the nature of the soul. Al-Kindi believed that reason and revelation need not conflict and that philosophical inquiry could support religious understanding.

He also touched on mental well-being. In a treatise sometimes referred to as *On the Device for Dispelling Sorrows*, Al-Kindi discussed how people might overcome grief and anxiety by proper reasoning and adjusting their perspectives. This anticipates ideas about cognitive approaches to emotional problems—namely, that challenging erroneous beliefs can relieve distress. Though he did not formalize this as a therapeutic system, his ideas show an early fusion of philosophical reasoning with concern for psychological states.

7.3.2. Al-Farabi: Combining Plato and Aristotle

Al-Farabi (c. 872–950) delved deeply into Plato's and Aristotle's philosophies, working to create a cohesive framework that integrated logic, metaphysics, politics, and psychology. He wrote commentaries and original treatises, attempting to show how these Greek systems could align with Islamic perspectives.

For instance, Al-Farabi proposed a theory of the **intellect** that drew from Aristotle but also included Neo-Platonic influences. He divided the intellect into several stages or levels: potential intellect, active intellect, acquired intellect, and so on. These gradations described how a human's mind could move from mere capacity to full understanding. Such distinctions influenced how later thinkers understood the development and function of rational thought.

Al-Farabi also wrote about the "virtuous city," inspired by Plato's *Republic*, suggesting that a just political structure mirrored the harmony of the individual soul. In these writings, we see a continuation of the Greek notion that psychological balance and ethical governance go hand in hand. By extension, it implied that personal mental health was connected to societal order—a perspective that would recur in various Islamic philosophical circles.

7.3.3. Avicenna (Ibn Sina): A Towering Polymath

Perhaps the most famous Islamic scholar who contributed to ideas related to the mind was **Avicenna** (in Arabic, Ibn Sina, 980–1037). He was a physician, philosopher, and prolific writer, known in the West largely for his medical encyclopedia, **The Canon of Medicine**, but also for major philosophical works like **The Book of Healing** (also known as *Kitab al-Shifa'*).

7.3.3.1. Avicenna's Psychology and the Soul

In *The Book of Healing*, Avicenna presented a detailed account of the soul's faculties, drawing on Aristotle but elaborating with his own insights. He described the internal senses—such as the common sense, imagination, estimation, and memory—in more systematic detail than many predecessors. Avicenna believed these inner senses worked with the external senses to process perceptions, store information, and generate thoughts.

He also introduced the famous "floating man" thought experiment. Imagine a person created in a state of perfect health and adult understanding, suspended in mid-air, deprived of any sensory input. Avicenna argued that this individual would still affirm his own existence, proving that self-awareness does not depend entirely on the physical senses. This was a crucial step in later discussions of consciousness and self-identity.

7.3.3.2. Medical and Psychological Insights

Avicenna's **Canon of Medicine** included chapters on mental health, describing conditions that resemble modern concepts of depression, mania, and anxiety. He recognized the importance of both physiological factors (e.g., humor imbalances) and psychological or environmental factors (e.g., life events, personal habits) in causing such disturbances. Avicenna recommended treatments that combined diet, medication, and what we might loosely call "therapeutic conversations."

He also developed an early understanding of psychosomatic effects, noting how mental states could influence physical health. Conversely, he saw how bodily imbalances could affect mood and cognition. This holistic view resonated with Galenic traditions yet showed unique advancements in categorizing and treating mental disorders.

7.3.4. Al-Ghazali: Theologian and Mystic

Al-Ghazali (1058–1111) was not a philosopher in the strict falasifa tradition; he was a theologian (mutakallim) and mystic (Sufi) who initially critiqued the philosophical approaches of Al-Farabi and Avicenna. His famous work *The Incoherence of the Philosophers* questioned the compatibility of certain Greek ideas with Islamic orthodoxy. Yet, Al-Ghazali contributed significantly to Islamic discussions about the human mind and spiritual well-being.

7.3.4.1. Emphasis on Spiritual Psychology

Al-Ghazali wrote extensively on inner purification, moral behavior, and the stages of spiritual growth. In works like *The Revival of the Religious Sciences (Ihya' Ulum al-Din)*, he described how the heart (qalb) can be cleansed of destructive emotions—envy, pride, greed—and filled with virtues like humility, gratitude, and love for God. This process involved reflective practices, remembrance of God (dhikr), and sincere repentance.

His understanding of the mind was inseparable from spirituality. While Avicenna approached psychology partly as a physician, Al-Ghazali approached it as a scholar of religion. He analyzed how illusions, self-deception, and worldly attachments cloud the intellect and disrupt emotional balance. His solutions were spiritual exercises, prayer, and detachment from excessive material concerns. Thus, Al-Ghazali brought a more religiously oriented psychological framework, one that deeply influenced later Islamic scholars.

7.3.4.2. Reconciling Rationalism and Spiritual Experience

Though critical of certain philosophical tenets, Al-Ghazali did not reject reason outright. He believed reason was a gift from God but that it had limits, especially concerning metaphysical truths and the direct experience of the divine. Mystical insight (or experiential knowledge) could go beyond rational argument. This perspective contributed to debates on how faith, reason, and the "heart's knowledge" interrelate—debates that included psychological questions about how humans acquire certainty or are transformed by spiritual experiences.

7.3.5. Averroes (Ibn Rushd) and the Latin West

Averroes (1126–1198), or Ibn Rushd, was a Cordoban philosopher and jurist who wrote extensive commentaries on Aristotle. While less focused on medical aspects than Avicenna, Averroes influenced Western Christian Scholastics, especially in the 13th century, when his commentaries were translated into Latin. He advanced detailed theories about intellect, advocating a view sometimes interpreted as a "universal intellect" shared by all humans—though modern scholars debate his exact meaning.

Regardless, Averroes's writings helped revive Aristotelianism in Western Europe. Thomas Aquinas and others engaged with Averroes's commentaries, whether to adopt or refute them. This cross-cultural interaction meant that Islamic philosophical explorations of the psyche filtered back into the Latin West, contributing to the Scholastic debates on the soul, reason, and free will.

7.4. Medical Institutions and Treatments for Mental Distress

7.4.1. Bimaristans and Compassionate Care

One important aspect of the Islamic Golden Age was the establishment of advanced hospitals, often called **bimaristans** (from the Persian *bimari* meaning "illness"). These institutions, funded by charitable endowments, provided care for patients regardless of background. Unlike many medieval European practices that treated the mentally ill with suspicion or harsh restraint, some bimaristans offered specialized wards for mental conditions.

Physicians in these hospitals employed holistic methods, combining herbal remedies, dietary regulation, talk-based interventions, and religious or spiritual comfort. While still grounded in humoral theory, they approached mental distress with a measure of empathy that stood out in the medieval world. Patients received baths, music therapy, and activities intended to stabilize their emotional states. Such efforts, while not "psychotherapy" in the modern sense, signaled a relatively progressive attitude toward mental healthcare.

7.4.2. Pioneers in Psychiatry

A few Islamic physicians, like **Al-Razi** (Rhazes, 865–925) and **Al-Majusi** (Haly Abbas, 10th century), wrote on mental disorders, describing symptoms akin to mania, depression, and even mania with psychosis. They advocated for what we might call early forms of behavioral observation: carefully noting a patient's daily habits, emotional triggers, and overall demeanor. Al-Razi, for example, emphasized building trust with the patient, reassuring them with logical arguments when they felt anxious or disturbed.

Though these treatments still relied on humoral explanations, the emphasis on observation, gentle methods, and an attempt at rational reassurance stands out. It suggests a nascent form of "therapeutic approach" where understanding the patient's mental state was as important as administering physical remedies.

7.5. Tensions Between Philosophy and Orthodoxy

While the Islamic Golden Age produced significant scholarship, it was not without conflicts. Religious conservatives worried that too much reliance on Greek philosophy could undermine Islamic teachings. Figures like Al-Ghazali criticized philosophers for straying from orthodoxy on matters like God's creation of the world or the immortality of the individual soul. Some philosophers, on the other hand, felt that reason, properly used, supported religious truth, though they sometimes diverged from strict literalism in interpreting sacred texts.

These tensions shaped how scholars wrote about the mind. Some pressed for purely rational, philosophical systems (heavily influenced by Aristotle and Neo-Platonism), while others emphasized the importance of revelation, mystical insight, and personal religious experience. In the 12th and 13th centuries, external pressures—like the Mongol invasions—also disrupted scholarly centers. Gradually, some of the intellectual dynamism shifted westward, into Islamic Spain and eventually back into Christian Europe.

7.6. The Enduring Impact on Western Thought

7.6.1. Transmission to Europe

As mentioned, Averroes's commentaries and Avicenna's treatises were translated into Latin, especially during the 12th-century Renaissance in Western Europe. Monks and scholars studied these works eagerly. Avicenna's medical texts, in particular, became standard references in European universities for centuries. His sections on mental disturbances influenced how later medieval physicians and Scholastic thinkers understood personality and mood disorders.

Moreover, the philosophical insights of Al-Farabi, Avicenna, and Averroes provided new angles on Aristotle. Latin Scholastics engaged with these commentaries, either to affirm or critique them, thereby refining their own ideas about the nature of the soul, intellect, and moral reasoning. Thomas Aquinas frequently cited "The Commentator" (Averroes) and "Avicenna," acknowledging the intellectual debt the Latin West owed to these Muslim scholars.

7.6.2. Lasting Legacy

Long after the Islamic Golden Age waned, its scholarly products continued to shape the conversation on mind and behavior. The holistic medical approaches, the classification of internal senses, and the use of reasoned argument to address emotional or spiritual distress laid groundwork that would be revisited during the Renaissance and beyond. Even as European thinkers moved toward more empirical methods, they built on a corpus of knowledge that had been safeguarded and expanded by Islamic civilization.

7.7. Other Centers of Islamic Scholarship

While Baghdad and Cordoba often get the spotlight, many other cities—Cairo, Damascus, Nishapur, Samarqand—hosted scholars who advanced knowledge of various disciplines. Libraries, translation centers, and teaching institutions flourished wherever stable governance and patronage existed. Consequently, the insights into psychology, broadly speaking, were never the product of a single location or moment. Rather, they emerged from a vast network of scholars who communicated across the Islamic world through letters, traveling teachers, and the pilgrimage routes.

7.8. Summary of the Islamic Approach to the Mind

The Islamic Golden Age offered:

1. **Preservation and Enhancement of Greek Ideas**: Scholars translated and elaborated upon Aristotle's and Galen's concepts, ensuring these did not vanish in the turmoil of the early Middle Ages.
2. **Philosophical Depth**: Thinkers like Al-Farabi and Avicenna developed intricate theories of the intellect and the inner senses, shaping future discussions on cognition and consciousness.
3. **Medical Advances**: Physicians like Avicenna and Al-Razi linked mental states with physiological conditions in a more detailed manner, creating proto-psychiatric approaches in bimaristans.
4. **Spiritual Integration**: Figures like Al-Ghazali combined theology, mysticism, and moral psychology, proposing ways to purify the heart and mind through spiritual discipline.
5. **Bridging Cultural Realms**: This scholarship circulated into Christian Europe, re-energizing philosophical and scientific studies there and laying groundwork for the later European Renaissance.

CHAPTER 8: THE RENAISSANCE AND HUMANISM

8.1. Setting the Stage

Spanning roughly from the 14th to the 17th centuries (though exact dates vary by region), the **Renaissance** was a time of rebirth in Europe, characterized by renewed interest in classical antiquity, new artistic achievements, and a gradual shift toward human-centered thinking. This era followed the Middle Ages, when Scholasticism dominated intellectual life under the oversight of the Catholic Church. As trade networks expanded, wealth accumulated in certain city-states—especially in Italy—enabling patrons to fund art, architecture, and scholarship.

The invention of the printing press in the mid-15th century accelerated the spread of ideas. Suddenly, texts could be reproduced in larger quantities, making ancient Greek and Roman writings more widely accessible. Translations from Arabic also became part of the textual mosaic. Against this backdrop, a movement called **Humanism** arose, emphasizing the study of classical languages, literature, history, and moral philosophy, all aiming to understand human nature and potential more directly than the medieval Scholastics had done.

This shift affected how scholars approached questions about the mind and behavior. While the theological perspective remained influential—Europe was still a predominantly Christian society—there was growing room for inquiries that focused on worldly life, individual experience, and empirical observation. This chapter will explore how the Renaissance and Humanism transformed conceptions of the mind, how these views intersected with art and literature, and how new scientific currents began sowing the seeds for later developments in psychology.

8.2. Renaissance Humanism

8.2.1. Return to Classical Sources

Renaissance Humanists believed that to unlock wisdom, one should return to the original Greek and Latin sources, bypassing medieval commentaries they deemed muddled. They studied authors like Plato, Aristotle, Cicero, and Seneca in their original languages rather than relying on potentially inaccurate translations. This philological work included comparing manuscripts, correcting errors, and seeking a purer understanding of ancient thought.

Francesco Petrarch (1304–1374) is often cited as an early Humanist. He admired classical writers and saw them as guides for moral and personal improvement. While Petrarch's own writings often dealt with personal introspection, love, and devotion, his emphasis on individual experience would be echoed in later writers who explored the mind as a distinct subject.

8.2.2. Civic Humanism and Education

In Italy, cities like Florence, Venice, and Rome were not only economic powers but cultural and intellectual centers. A notion called "civic humanism" took root, which argued that studying classical texts was not merely for personal edification but for the betterment of society. By understanding historical examples of virtue, leadership, and rhetoric, citizens could shape more just and prosperous communities.

Education, or "studia humanitatis," encompassed grammar, rhetoric, poetry, moral philosophy, and history. The rationale was that cultivating eloquent, well-rounded individuals led to a virtuous and effective civic life. Although these subjects might seem tangential to psychology, the underlying premise was that knowledge of language, literature, and ethics refines the human mind, making it more rational, empathetic, and capable of discernment. Such an approach implicitly recognized that mental faculties can be developed and improved—an idea that would resonate in later educational and psychological theories.

8.2.3. Erasmus and Thomas More

Desiderius Erasmus (c. 1466–1536) embodied the Humanist spirit, traveling widely across Europe and publishing critical editions of ancient texts. Erasmus satirized the follies of his time in works like *In Praise of Folly*, poking fun at superstitions and clerical abuses. He believed in reforming the Church from within, emphasizing inner devotion and moral renewal over empty ritual. In psychological terms, Erasmus advocated for guiding individuals—through education and reflection—to align their minds with virtues of compassion and rational piety.

Thomas More (1478–1535), in his book *Utopia*, envisaged an ideal society where reason and communal welfare took precedence over greed and power struggles. Although *Utopia* is partly satire, it hints at how some Humanists believed rational design could shape human behavior for the better. This focus on the mind's malleability through social systems, laws, and education pointed toward a more secular approach to shaping human conduct—though More himself was devoutly Catholic.

8.3. The Flourishing of Arts and Its Psychological Significance

8.3.1. Renaissance Art and the Human Form

The Renaissance is famous for its artistic achievements, including paintings, sculptures, and architecture that celebrated the beauty of the human body. Artists like **Leonardo da Vinci (1452–1519)**, **Michelangelo (1475–1564)**, and **Raphael (1483–1520)** studied anatomy to depict figures with unprecedented realism. This interest in accurately portraying human form reflected a broader cultural shift that elevated the human experience itself as a worthy subject.

Leonardo da Vinci's notebooks contain anatomical drawings and speculations on perception, vision, and the role of the brain in controlling the body. Though he wasn't a "psychologist," his curiosity about how sensations enter the mind or how emotions manifest in facial expressions showed a budding empirical approach to understanding human nature. Renaissance art, by focusing so closely on individual expression, also implied recognition of distinct personalities, emotions, and mental states worthy of depiction.

8.3.2. Portraiture and Individual Identity

In the Middle Ages, art often served didactic religious purposes—saints, biblical scenes, and iconography. Renaissance portraiture, however, gave new prominence to individual identity. Patrons wanted paintings that captured their unique features, personalities, and status. This shift paralleled the Humanist focus on individual dignity and potential.

From a psychological standpoint, the emphasis on portraiture could be seen as an early form of exploring personal identity. Artists like Jan van Eyck in Northern Europe meticulously represented their subjects' facial details, attire, and emotional nuances. In Italy, Mona Lisa's mysterious smile incited speculation about her thoughts and feelings. Such attention to the subjective interior of the sitter hinted at the complexity of human psychology and how it might be represented visually.

8.4. Scientific Undercurrents and Challenges to Orthodoxy

8.4.1. Moving Beyond Scholasticism

While Scholasticism did not instantly disappear, Renaissance scholars criticized what they saw as overly technical and abstract debates about arcane theological points. The new spirit favored direct observation and critical analysis of natural phenomena. This attitude foreshadowed the Scientific Revolution, which would gain momentum in the 16th and 17th centuries.

Some early attempts at systematic observation included **Andreas Vesalius's (1514–1564)** anatomical studies, published in *De humani corporis fabrica* (1543). Vesalius dissected human cadavers—something still controversial at the time—and corrected longstanding errors in Galen's anatomy. Though his focus was the body, he also examined the brain, cranial nerves, and the nervous system. By providing more accurate anatomical data, Vesalius set a precedent for relying on empirical evidence rather than dogmatic repetition of ancient texts.

8.4.2. The Role of Astronomy and Empiricism

Astronomy might seem distant from psychology, but the intellectual shift in that domain had broad consequences for how people approached knowledge in general. **Nicolaus Copernicus (1473–1543)** challenged the geocentric model, proposing that the Earth and planets revolve around the Sun. Such challenges to Aristotelian cosmology mirrored challenges to medieval Scholastic frameworks for understanding reality. If the Earth itself was not at the center of the universe, might the mind also not revolve around preconceived dogmas?

Over time, these scientific upheavals encouraged a mindset that demanded direct observation, experimentation, and a willingness to revise beliefs. This new methodology, though not yet fully applied to studying the mind, laid the groundwork for later scientific psychology. Renaissance thinkers were planting seeds: the same approach that questioned the absolute authority of theological or classical texts might someday question assumptions about human perception, cognition, and behavior.

8.5. Innovations in Literature and the Inner Self

8.5.1. Shakespeare and the Complexity of Characters

In literature, the Renaissance saw playwrights like **William Shakespeare (1564–1616)** portray characters with striking psychological depth. Works such as *Hamlet*, *Macbeth*, and *Othello* explore internal conflicts, madness, ambition, guilt, and love, all while diving into the minds of their protagonists and antagonists. While not systematic psychology, these plays reflect an intuitive understanding that human behavior arises from complex mental and emotional processes.

Shakespeare's soliloquies, for example, show characters debating with themselves, revealing their fears, hopes, and rationalizations. The public devoured these portrayals, showing a growing cultural appetite for nuanced representations of interior life. This dramatic literature indirectly pushed the concept that the human psyche is layered, conflicted, and shaped by both rational thought and emotional turmoil—an idea that would echo in the future development of psychology.

8.5.2. Montaigne's Essays

Michel de Montaigne (1533–1592), a French writer, is known for his *Essais* (Essays), in which he reflected candidly on his own thoughts, experiences, and beliefs. Montaigne questioned absolute certainty, championed skepticism about human knowledge, and probed the variability of human customs. He wrote about his personal fears, his behavior, and even bodily functions with frankness rare for his time.

In many ways, Montaigne's introspection built on Augustine's confessional style but diverged by focusing less on sin and salvation and more on the variety of human existence. His approach resonated with the Renaissance spirit of self-discovery and critical thinking. He recognized that knowledge of oneself could be an endless journey, echoing an early "psychological" perspective: the self is a legitimate subject for observation and reflection, independent of purely religious frameworks.

8.6. Humanist Education and the Shaping of Character

8.6.1. Educating the Whole Person

Humanist educators believed in cultivating virtue, wisdom, and eloquence in students. Figures like **Vittorino da Feltre (1378–1446)** set up schools where children learned both classical languages and moral philosophy alongside physical exercise—aiming for a balanced development of body and mind. The underlying assumption was that individuals could be shaped to become rational, ethical members of society if guided correctly.

Such an educational philosophy touches on psychological ideas about learning and development. Instead of focusing solely on theological doctrines, Humanist pedagogy emphasized classical moral lessons and a broad curriculum. This implied an early recognition that environment, teaching methods, and exposure to culture significantly influence how the mind develops—a principle that aligns with later conceptions of "nurture" in the nature vs. nurture debate.

8.6.2. Women in Humanist Education

Although Renaissance Europe was largely patriarchal, a few women from affluent or noble families received humanist educations and contributed intellectually. **Isotta Nogarola (1418–1466)**, for instance, engaged in dialogues about theological and moral issues, while **Cassandra Fedele (1465–1558)** excelled in public orations and Latin letters. These women's works, although not explicitly psychological, challenged assumptions about women's intellectual capacity. They suggested that differences in achievements might result not from inherent limitations but from unequal educational opportunities—a view that would echo in later discussions about intellectual development and gender.

8.7. Religious Upheavals and Their Psychological Implications

8.7.1. The Reformation

While not strictly part of the Renaissance, the **Protestant Reformation** in the 16th century deeply altered Europe's religious and cultural landscape. Initiated by figures like Martin Luther (1483–1546) and John Calvin (1509–1564), the Reformation questioned the authority and practices of the Catholic Church. It emphasized individual faith and the direct reading of scripture.

From a psychological standpoint, this shift placed more responsibility on the individual's conscience. Faith became more personal, sometimes increasing introspection and anxiety about salvation. The notion of "faith alone" could intensify internal guilt or self-examination, reflecting how religious changes can alter one's mental framework. Meanwhile, Catholic responses in the **Counter-Reformation** also adapted, with orders like the Jesuits focusing heavily on disciplined education, spiritual exercises, and reflection. These movements, on both sides, underscored the significance of personal conviction and mental commitment, weaving theology and a kind of proto-psychology together.

8.7.2. Mysticism and Interior Devotion

Across Europe, a wave of mysticism and devotional movements paralleled the official Reformation and Counter-Reformation. Individuals like **Teresa of Ávila (1515–1582)** and **John of the Cross (1542–1591)**, within Catholic Spain, wrote about spiritual ecstasy, prayer, and the "dark night of the soul." They examined how the mind and will navigate divine union or wrestle with spiritual dryness.

Teresa's *Interior Castle* mapped stages of prayer as rooms in a castle, each step revealing deeper layers of the soul's experience. Such an allegory offered a psychological dimension to spiritual progression, suggesting that one's internal faculties and desires evolve through concentrated practice and grace. Though firmly within religious context, these texts contributed to a broader understanding of how mental focus, emotional states, and beliefs interplay.

8.8. Seeds of Future Scientific Exploration of the Mind

8.8.1. Empiricism's Emergence

As the Renaissance advanced, some thinkers started leaning more toward empirical methods. While still not recognized as "psychologists," individuals such as **Francis Bacon (1561-1626)** promoted inductive reasoning: collecting observations to form general conclusions, rather than relying on deductive logic from assumed first principles. Bacon criticized Scholastic debates for being detached from real-world investigation. His approach foreshadowed the scientific method that would shape modern psychology centuries later.

8.8.2. Mechanical Philosophy and the Body-Mind Question

Toward the end of the Renaissance, new mechanical philosophies began describing nature in terms of matter and motion. Philosophers such as **René Descartes (1596-1650)**—who properly belongs to the early modern period—questioned the nature of reality and laid the groundwork for mind-body dualism. Though Descartes's major works emerged after the Renaissance prime, the cultural shift of the era prepared the stage for his ideas. With increased emphasis on observation and logic, people were more willing to challenge established authorities, including the Church and Aristotle. This environment made space for radical rethinking of how the mind might relate to the physical body, setting the scene for future psychological debates.

8.9. Summarizing Renaissance Contributions to Psychology

1. **Human-Centered Inquiry**: Renaissance Humanism turned attention back to the classical ideal of nurturing well-rounded individuals. Moral and psychological discussions became less purely theological and more focused on human capacities and experiences in this life.
2. **Rediscovery of Classical Texts**: By returning to Greek and Roman sources in their original languages, Humanists helped ensure ancient theories of the soul, reason, and virtue were

more accurately understood. This corrected some medieval misinterpretations and introduced new dialogues about mental faculties.
3. **Artistic Depictions of the Inner Life**: Renaissance art, literature, and theater began representing people with emotional complexity, suggesting an evolving understanding of the psyche as nuanced and worthy of detailed study or portrayal.
4. **Early Empirical Tendencies**: Innovations in anatomy, astronomy, and natural philosophy promoted observation and critical thinking. While not directly forming "psychology," these approaches hinted that the mind could also be studied more systematically in the future.
5. **Educational Reform**: Humanist schools and tutors championed the idea that the mind is malleable, shaped by learning and environment, laying groundwork for later debates on how best to foster intellectual and moral development.

8.10. Limitations and Lasting Influence

Despite these developments, Renaissance Europe did not produce a formalized science of psychology. Alchemy, astrology, and humoral theory remained widespread, and theological explanations still held strong sway. Many breakthroughs were in the arts and philology rather than in structured experiments on human cognition or emotion. Nonetheless, the Renaissance established essential preconditions:

- A revived confidence in human reason and potential.
- Wider availability of texts, thanks to the printing press.
- Growing curiosity about the natural world, including the human body and mind.

By the end of the 16th century, intellectual currents were shifting more decisively toward observational methods and the beginnings of the scientific revolution. The stage was set for figures like Descartes, Galileo, and others to push beyond scholastic and purely classical boundaries, questioning everything from the cosmos to consciousness. Psychology would remain entangled with philosophy for some time, but the seeds for its eventual split into a separate discipline were being planted.

8.11. Transition to Enlightenment and Empiricism

As we move forward, the next phase—often labeled the **Age of Enlightenment**—would see philosophers in Europe turn a sharper eye toward the mechanisms of knowledge, the structure of society, and the role of experience in shaping the mind. Thinkers like John Locke would champion empiricism, insisting that knowledge arises from sensory inputs. Others, like Descartes and Leibniz, would push rationalist arguments. These debates would lay the intellectual scaffolding for psychology as an empirical science, though that formalization would not come until the late 19th century.

In the next chapter, we will explore how Enlightenment philosophers deepened or challenged the Renaissance legacies, setting up new frameworks for interpreting perception, cognition, and human nature. We will see how empirical experiments in physics and physiology—mirroring the new scientific spirit—started to inform discussions about the senses, setting the stage for psychophysics and the eventual birth of modern psychology.

CHAPTER 9: THE AGE OF ENLIGHTENMENT AND EMPIRICISM

9.1. The Enlightenment

By the late 17th and throughout the 18th century, Europe underwent profound intellectual changes that would later be called the **Enlightenment**. This period was fueled by confidence in human reason and an emerging belief in progress. Traditional sources of authority—particularly ecclesiastical and monarchical—were increasingly questioned. Scholars and philosophically inclined writers challenged doctrines that had gone largely unexamined during the medieval era. As new scientific discoveries became known to a wider public, many concluded that reason, observation, and systematic inquiry could uncover truths not only about the physical world but also about human nature.

This attitude was fed by the successes of the **Scientific Revolution**, which had begun earlier with figures like Galileo and Kepler, and reached new heights with Isaac Newton's formulation of universal gravitation in the late 17th century. If mathematical laws could explain planetary motion, it seemed plausible that equally discoverable laws might govern society, morality, and even the human mind. The Enlightenment thus expanded beyond natural science, seeking rational principles for virtually every domain of life, from government to education to personal conduct.

Within this broad context, thinkers refined or challenged earlier views on the mind. The concept of "empiricism" emerged in contrast to older or more rationalist traditions, arguing that experience, particularly sense experience, is the ultimate foundation of knowledge. This emphasis on observation and experience influenced how people thought about learning, perception, and the formation of ideas. It also laid the groundwork for a more "scientific" approach to mental phenomena, even if formal scientific psychology would not appear until centuries later.

9.2. Historical Backdrop

9.2.1. Political and Social Changes

The Enlightenment did not erupt suddenly; it was shaped by turbulent events. The Thirty Years' War (1618–1648) devastated much of Central Europe, prompting reflection on religious conflicts and the powers of monarchs. In England, the mid-17th-century Civil War and the later Glorious Revolution (1688) led to a constitutional monarchy that favored certain civil liberties and parliamentary authority. These political transformations fueled debates about individual rights, social contracts, and the nature of human beings: Were people naturally good, evil, or something in between? How did they form societies and govern themselves?

Such questions intersected with emerging ideas about human psychology and motivation. Writers increasingly speculated about whether moral behavior sprang from innate principles (perhaps installed by God) or from empirical experiences (habits, learning, environmental influences). The Enlightenment was not a single, uniform movement. It varied by region—France, Britain, Germany, and other nations had their own Enlightenment contexts—but it shared an overarching faith in human reason and a willingness to critique received wisdom.

9.2.2. The Scientific Influence

The new respect for empirical evidence was strongly tied to the achievements of scientists who used systematic experimentation and mathematics to study physical phenomena. Galileo's telescopic observations challenged geocentrism. Newton's *Principia Mathematica* (1687) demonstrated that universal laws—expressible in precise mathematical terms—could explain both celestial and earthly motion. Such breakthroughs weakened the traditional reliance on Aristotelian physics and Scholastic philosophy.

Inspired by these successes, intellectuals asked whether a similar approach could clarify complex questions about learning, moral development, and the workings of the mind. Could "laws" of thought or behavior be discovered? Could philosophers or "natural philosophers" (the term then used for scientists) provide a framework that explained how people process information, form beliefs, and develop ethical norms? While they lacked sophisticated scientific tools for studying the brain or conducting experiments on cognition, Enlightenment thinkers laid the conceptual foundations for future inquiries.

9.3. The Rise of Empiricism

9.3.1. Defining Empiricism

Empiricism, as a broad philosophical stance, posits that sense experience is the primary or only source of genuine knowledge. In other words, we learn about the world by seeing, hearing, touching, tasting, and smelling it, then reflecting on or reasoning about these experiences. This stood in contrast to **rationalism**, which held that some truths are accessible through pure reason or innate ideas, independent of sensory input.

During the Enlightenment, empiricism aligned well with the new scientific spirit. Empirical methods in physics, chemistry, and biology seemed to confirm the power of careful observation and experimentation. Consequently, empiricist philosophers claimed that the mind itself, rather than being furnished with inborn concepts, begins more like a blank slate (in Latin, *tabula rasa*). Our experiences mark this slate with impressions that combine to form ideas. This viewpoint would become crucial for understanding how learning and perception might shape character, beliefs, and knowledge.

9.3.2. Francis Bacon: Laying the Groundwork

Though Francis Bacon (1561–1626) lived before the height of the Enlightenment, he heavily influenced Enlightenment empiricism. Bacon rejected the Scholastic approach of deducing truths primarily from established authorities or from pure logic. Instead, he advocated for **inductive reasoning**: collecting data from particular instances and gradually forming broader generalizations or laws.

In works like *Novum Organum* (1620), Bacon detailed the "idols" (errors) that mislead the mind—idols of the tribe (human nature biases), idols of the cave (individual biases), idols of the marketplace (language and social interaction distortions), and idols of the theater (dogmatic philosophical systems). By identifying these errors, Bacon hoped to refine the process of knowledge acquisition. Although he did not produce a theory of psychology as such, his method underscored the importance of empirical observation and systematic doubt about preconceived notions. This shaped later Enlightenment thinkers who studied human cognition and behavior.

9.3.3. Thomas Hobbes: Mechanistic Interpretation of Mind

Thomas Hobbes (1588–1679), an English philosopher best known for his political treatise *Leviathan* (1651), also contributed to Enlightenment approaches to the mind. Influenced by the Scientific

Revolution, Hobbes treated human thought as matter in motion, akin to physical processes. He considered sensations the result of mechanical interactions between external objects and the sense organs, which then produce "motions" in the brain.

Hobbes's mechanistic view implied that all mental contents have physical origins. Complex ideas, he argued, emerge from simpler ones as the brain rearranges these motions. For Hobbes, imagination is the decaying sense after the external object is gone, and memory is a weaker continuation of that same process. This thoroughly naturalistic account contrasted sharply with earlier medieval or religious conceptions of the soul as something immaterial. Though Hobbes did not fully develop a psychology, his insistence on a natural, mechanistic explanation for mental phenomena echoed Enlightenment attitudes that placed human cognition squarely within the realm of scientific study.

9.3.4. Pierre Gassendi and the Atomistic Mind

Another figure bridging the gap between the Scientific Revolution and Enlightenment thought was **Pierre Gassendi** (1592–1655), a French philosopher who revived Epicurean atomism in the modern era. Gassendi proposed that everything, including the mind, consists of atoms in motion. He challenged Cartesian dualism by denying an immaterial "thinking substance" separate from matter. Instead, Gassendi saw consciousness as an emergent property of physical processes, an idea that would later surface in discussions on materialism and sensationalism.

Though overshadowed historically by Descartes, Gassendi's materialist perspective resonated with certain Enlightenment thinkers who believed that mental events must be explained by reference to the physical body and sensory experiences. His stance anticipated debates on how to reconcile consciousness with material processes—an ongoing philosophical and scientific question.

9.4. Enlightenment Salons, Academies, and Public Sphere

9.4.1. Salons and Coffeehouses

During the 18th century, intellectual exchange moved beyond universities or royal courts into more informal venues like **salons** (especially in France) and **coffeehouses** (particularly in England). Wealthy hostesses in Paris organized salons where philosophers (called "philosophes") gathered to discuss ideas, critique each other's works, and debate politics, religion, science, and human nature. In England, coffeehouses played a similar role, offering a public space where people from different social strata could meet, read newspapers, and converse about current events.

This culture of open debate fostered a sense that human knowledge was something to be collectively refined. Many participants were not professional scholars but educated citizens and writers—suggesting that the mind's pursuit of truth was a communal enterprise. Philosophical and pseudo-psychological discussions mixed freely with gossip, political argument, and literary criticism. While not "research" in a formal sense, these gatherings spread Enlightenment ideals and shaped how ordinary people understood the mind's capacity for reason.

9.4.2. Scientific Societies and Academies

Parallel to these informal gatherings, more structured scientific academies formed, like the **Royal Society** in London (founded 1660) and the **Académie des Sciences** in Paris (founded 1666). Members conducted experiments, published findings, and advanced a rigorous methodology for investigating the natural world. Although their early focus was on physics, astronomy, and chemistry, the principle of collaborative empirical inquiry would eventually influence how people approached topics like human anatomy, physiology, and the nervous system—laying stepping stones for the later scientific study of mental processes.

The academy culture prized demonstration and reproducible evidence, shaping an Enlightenment mindset that was impatient with dogmatic claims unsupported by experiment. Over time, as physiology advanced, thinkers began to wonder if the same empirical rules applied to understanding sensation, memory, and even consciousness. While these ideas remained speculative in the 18th century, the shift in cultural attitudes was crucial. By normalizing the pursuit of data-driven conclusions, academies contributed to the environment in which psychology could someday emerge as an empirical science.

9.5. French Philosophes

9.5.1. Voltaire and the Critique of Dogma

Voltaire (1694–1778), the pen name of François-Marie Arouet, was a leading figure among the French philosophes. Although not a systematic philosopher of mind, Voltaire took inspiration from Locke's empiricism and from Newtonian science, promoting religious toleration and rational critique of superstition. In works like *Letters on England*, he praised English intellectual freedom and highlighted Locke's ideas about the mind as shaped by experience.

Voltaire's influence was less about new psychological theories and more about championing freedom of thought, skepticism toward authority, and the idea that reason and observation should guide inquiry. His witty attacks on dogma and fanaticism shaped public discourse, encouraging a mentality that tested beliefs against common sense and evidence. This environment nurtured the notion that the mind can be studied as a natural phenomenon rather than an inscrutable mystery protected by religious doctrine.

9.5.2. Diderot's Encyclopédie: Spreading Knowledge

Denis Diderot (1713–1784), co-editor of the massive *Encyclopédie*, shared the Enlightenment passion for cataloging all human knowledge. While covering subjects ranging from metallurgy to music, the *Encyclopédie* also included entries on logic, perception, and human development. Diderot was influenced by Locke's and Condillac's empirical theories of mind, viewing understanding as built from sensations.

Diderot flirted with materialist ideas: the possibility that all mental faculties result from physical processes in the brain. He questioned whether an immortal soul or purely spiritual substance was necessary to explain thought. In private writings, Diderot speculated that the senses and social environment might fully account for human personality, morality, and even genius. Though this stance was controversial, the *Encyclopédie* project as a whole promoted a spirit of open inquiry, highlighting how empirical or materialist explanations for mental phenomena could be discussed alongside traditional views.

9.5.3. Étienne Bonnot de Condillac: Sensationalism

Perhaps the most explicitly psychological of the French Enlightenment thinkers was **Étienne Bonnot de Condillac** (1714–1780). In his *Treatise on Sensations* (1754), Condillac built on Locke's empirical premise but pushed it further. He proposed that all mental faculties—memory, judgment, imagination, even the sense of self—arise from transformed sensations. To illustrate this, he famously used the metaphor of a statue with no senses, gradually acquiring them one by one. Each new sense introduced fresh experiences, which the mind then combined, compared, and connected to form complex ideas.

Condillac's emphasis on "sensation" as the sole foundation of mental life is sometimes called **sensationalism**. He argued that the statue, endowed first with smell, then hearing, then sight, etc., would develop the ability to compare sensations, form notions of space, time, and eventually more abstract ideas. Condillac's approach effectively made psychology a branch of epistemology: to understand how knowledge forms, one must see how raw sensory data become ideas.

This perspective mirrored the Enlightenment's broader optimism about the malleability of the human mind. If all ideas come from experience, then changing educational methods, social conditions, and moral teachings can transform individuals and societies. Condillac's sensationalism would resonate with later philosophers and early psychologists who tried to ground mental phenomena in observable processes, though it also faced criticism from rationalists who believed certain concepts (like mathematical truths) were not derivable from mere sensory impressions.

9.6. Beyond France

9.6.1. Christian Wolff and German Rationalism

In German-speaking regions, Enlightenment thought developed with a strong rationalist flavor influenced by Gottfried Wilhelm Leibniz (1646–1716). **Christian Wolff** (1679–1754) systematized Leibniz's ideas in a grand philosophical architecture that blended reason and metaphysics. Though Wolff was more rationalist than empiricist, he wrote about psychology, coining terms such as "empirical psychology" and "rational psychology." Empirical psychology, in Wolff's view, involved observing mental events, while rational psychology tried to deduce fundamental truths about the soul's nature.

Wolff's approach introduced a more formal classification for studying the mind, naming faculties like sensibility, understanding, and will. While he did not conduct experiments, the very notion that psychology might exist as a separate discipline—split into empirical and rational parts—foreshadowed future developments. Wolff's works influenced German universities, prompting them to include "psychology" as a subject within philosophy, albeit in a proto-scientific form.

9.6.2. Immanuel Kant's Critical Turn (Prelude)

Though Immanuel Kant (1724–1804) belongs partly to a post-Enlightenment or "late Enlightenment" period, his critical philosophy emerged in response to both rationalism and empiricism. Without preempting the next phases in the story, we can note that Kant questioned whether pure experience or pure reason alone was sufficient for knowledge. He suggested the mind comes equipped with innate categories that structure sensory input. This position foreshadowed the tension between empirical psychology and claims of inbuilt cognitive structures—an issue that remains important in modern debates.

Kant was skeptical that psychology could become a rigorous science akin to physics, because mental phenomena do not easily lend themselves to mathematical measurement and lack external spatial extension. Nevertheless, his critiques spurred others to refine their methods, eventually leading to developments in psychophysics and experimental approaches in the 19th century. For the Enlightenment context, Kant's work represented the culmination of efforts to understand how reason and experience interact in forming knowledge.

9.7. Impact on Education, Ethics, and Society

9.7.1. The Educational Impulse

One major outcome of Enlightenment empiricism was a renewed focus on **education** as a tool for shaping individuals and improving society. If human minds are molds shaped by experiences, then controlling the "input" might produce better citizens. Figures like John Locke (whom we will examine in Chapter 10) advocated for gentle, reason-based instruction that nurtured a child's developing faculties. Jean-Jacques Rousseau (1712–1778), though not strictly an empiricist, wrote *Émile* (1762), describing an educational scheme that emphasizes direct experience and minimal interference by adults.

Even if Rousseau's view was more romantic or naturalistic than the mainstream Enlightenment stance, it showed the era's shared assumption: the environment shapes mental development. This assumption encouraged the creation of new schools, teaching methods, and social reforms aimed at cultivating rational, responsible members of society. As such, the Enlightenment concept of the mind—flexible, shaped by experience, and guided by reason—had tangible effects on how children were taught and how moral training was approached.

9.7.2. Moral Psychology and Social Theories

Enlightenment discourse often combined morality with theories of human nature. Some thinkers proposed **moral sense** theories, suggesting that humans possess an innate capacity for empathy or benevolence. Others, leaning on Hobbes's or Locke's ideas, argued that morals come from social contracts or habit formation. Enlightenment authors generally believed that reason could discern ethical truths or at least weigh the social consequences of behavior. They debated whether moral sentiments arose purely from self-interest or if there were more altruistic motives in the human psyche.

These discussions influenced how societies framed laws and governance. Enlightenment ideals called for rational justice systems, less reliance on torture or spectacle, and a focus on shaping citizens who behaved ethically due to reasoned conviction rather than fear. In short, the Enlightenment saw the mind as an integral part of progress—if one could understand and direct mental processes, one could create a more enlightened, just society.

9.8. Challenges and Critiques

9.8.1. Rationalists vs. Empiricists

While many Enlightenment thinkers embraced empiricism, not everyone agreed. Rationalists argued that certain truths—like basic principles of logic or mathematics—could not come from mere sensory experience. In addition, some religious philosophers maintained that moral truths or the concept of God required innate ideas or special revelation. The debate between rationalism and empiricism thus drove philosophical discussion throughout the Enlightenment, leading to notable works by Descartes, Spinoza, Leibniz, Locke, Berkeley, and Hume—each claiming different balances of reason and experience in forming knowledge.

9.8.2. Materialism and Spiritual Concerns

Another tension arose between **materialists**—who believed everything, including mind, could be explained by physical processes—and those who upheld the spiritual or immaterial nature of the soul. Materialists like La Mettrie (author of *Man a Machine*, 1747) provoked controversies by suggesting that mental processes were purely mechanical. Religious authorities and many philosophers reacted strongly, fearing that if the soul were denied, moral responsibility might collapse. This clash underscored that Enlightenment openness to new ideas sometimes ran headlong into deeply rooted religious and ethical convictions.

9.8.3. Social Limitations

Despite Enlightenment talk of universal reason and human rights, many thinkers did not extend these ideals to all groups. Women, lower-class individuals, and colonized peoples were often excluded from full participation in the "Republic of Letters," and some Enlightenment figures espoused hierarchical or even racist views that justified European imperialism. These contradictions remind us that while the Enlightenment advanced certain kinds of freedom and knowledge, it remained shaped by existing social biases.

9.9. The Enlightenment's Psychological Legacy

The Enlightenment's pursuit of knowledge through reason, observation, and debate profoundly influenced the future of psychology. Key legacies include:

1. **Empirical Attitude**: The emphasis on sense experience as the basis for understanding the mind laid a conceptual framework that would eventually inspire experimental psychology.
2. **Focus on Education and Environment**: If individuals are formed by their experiences, interventions in schooling, social settings, and moral development can transform them—an idea that underlies many later psychological theories about the power of upbringing and culture.
3. **Naturalization of Mental Processes**: Philosophers like Hobbes and Gassendi treated thinking as a physical or mechanical phenomenon, challenging the older notion of the soul as purely supernatural. This trend continued in 19th-century physiological studies of the nervous system.
4. **Public Sphere of Intellectual Debate**: Salons, coffeehouses, and academies promoted the idea that knowledge about mind and behavior could be openly discussed and refined, not just left to religious or philosophical authorities.

CHAPTER 10: EARLY MODERN PHILOSOPHERS

10.1. Introduction

The period broadly covering the 17th and 18th centuries saw an explosion of philosophical inquiry that laid the groundwork for contemporary thought on the mind. Among the many influential figures of this era, **René Descartes**, **John Locke**, and **David Hume** stand out for their profound influence on how we conceptualize consciousness, knowledge, and personal identity. Each approached the mind from a distinct angle—Descartes focusing on rationalist dualism, Locke on empirical foundations of ideas, and Hume on skepticism about causation and the self. Their debates continue to echo in modern philosophy, cognitive science, and psychology.

In this chapter, we will delve into the lives and key works of these three pivotal thinkers. We will see how Descartes introduced a radical separation between mind and body while also pioneering new methods of doubt. Then we will explore how Locke's empiricism reoriented philosophical discussions around the idea of a mind shaped by experiences. Finally, we will examine Hume's formidable skepticism, which cast doubt on our assumptions about causality, the self, and even the certainty of reason itself.

10.2. René Descartes

10.2.1. Background and Method

René Descartes was a French philosopher and mathematician often called the "Father of Modern Philosophy." Educated in the Scholastic tradition, he became dissatisfied with many of its assumptions. Descartes sought a fresh method that could yield certain knowledge, akin to the mathematical proofs he admired. In his seminal work, *Meditations on First Philosophy* (1641), he introduced a method of systematic doubt—questioning everything that could possibly be doubted until he reached something indubitable.

This approach led to his famous conclusion, "Cogito, ergo sum" ("I think, therefore I am"). Even if he doubted the existence of the external world or the reliability of his senses, Descartes believed the act of doubting proved the existence of a thinking entity—himself as a "res cogitans" (thinking thing). This marked a turning point, as it shifted the foundation of knowledge to the individual's self-awareness rather than external authority or tradition.

10.2.2. Mind-Body Dualism

Descartes proposed a **dualist** framework: the mind (or soul) is a non-extended, thinking substance, while the body is an extended, non-thinking substance. Thus, mind and body are fundamentally different in essence. How they interact became the famous "mind-body problem." Descartes hypothesized that the pineal gland in the brain might be the locus of this interaction, though he offered no detailed physiological mechanism.

This mind-body distinction set the stage for centuries of debate in psychology and philosophy. On one hand, Descartes's dualism allowed for a realm of subjective consciousness not reducible to physical laws. On the other hand, it introduced the challenge of explaining how a non-physical mind influences physical processes. Later thinkers, from materialists to behaviorists, would reject this stark dualism, arguing that it either complicates scientific investigation or fails to explain mental phenomena in a naturalistic way.

10.2.3. Innate Ideas and Rationalism

Descartes also believed in **innate ideas**—concepts that exist in the mind independent of sensory experience. Examples he gave include the idea of God, mathematical truths, and logical principles. For Descartes, sense data might be helpful but could be deceptive; the truest knowledge arises from the mind's rational insight into these innate concepts. This stance aligns with rationalism: the idea that reason can yield certain truths that sensory experience cannot fully justify.

In future psychology, debates about whether certain cognitive structures or concepts are inborn or learned would draw on Cartesian arguments. Much later, Noam Chomsky's theory of an innate language faculty in the 20th century can be seen as echoing a rationalist approach, though obviously in a more empirically informed context. Descartes's emphasis on the thinking self as the core of knowledge also contributed to introspectionism in early psychological science, where researchers tried to analyze their own conscious processes as data.

10.2.4. Implications for Early Psychology

Although Descartes was not an experimental psychologist, his theories had multiple implications:

1. **Focus on Consciousness**: By emphasizing the thinking self, he reinforced the study of subjective awareness as a key to understanding human nature.
2. **Mechanistic Physiology**: Even though the mind was non-physical, Descartes saw the body as a machine that follows physical laws. He dissected animals, speculated about reflexes, and contributed to an early mechanistic view of physiological processes.

3. **Mind-Body Problem**: The strict dualism invited future inquiry about how mental and physical realms relate, a question that remains central in philosophy of mind and certain branches of psychology.

10.3. John Locke

10.3.1. Historical Context and Influence

John Locke was an English philosopher, political theorist, and physician. His era was shaped by England's Civil War, the Glorious Revolution, and the ascendancy of constitutional government. Locke's experiences in politics and medicine influenced his approach to philosophy, emphasizing observation, practical reason, and the consent of the governed. He admired the empirical spirit championed by Bacon and the scientific achievements exemplified by Robert Boyle and Isaac Newton.

Locke's greatest philosophical work, *An Essay Concerning Human Understanding* (1690), laid out a systematic account of how human beings acquire knowledge. His arguments had wide-ranging effects, shaping the British Empiricist tradition and influencing Enlightenment thinkers across Europe. Figures like Voltaire and the American Founding Fathers cited Locke's ideas on government and the mind, demonstrating his broad appeal.

10.3.2. The Mind as a Blank Slate (*Tabula Rasa*)

Locke famously rejected Descartes's doctrine of innate ideas, insisting that all knowledge derives from experience. According to Locke, when a child is born, their mind is like white paper void of characters: a *tabula rasa*. Over time, sensory impressions (what Locke called "sensation") and internal operations of the mind (which he called "reflection") generate simple ideas. Complex ideas then form by combining, relating, or abstracting these simpler elements.

In Locke's view, no principles—whether moral, mathematical, or religious—are inherently stamped into the mind at birth. Instead, the environment and experiences shape each person's concepts. This idea significantly impacted educational theory and moral philosophy. If individuals are shaped by environment, it follows that social structures, teaching methods, and personal habits can transform one's character and intellectual capacity.

10.3.3. Types of Ideas and Quality Distinctions

Locke distinguished between **simple** and **complex** ideas:

- **Simple Ideas**: The building blocks of thought, acquired passively through sensation (colors, shapes, tastes, sounds) or reflection (the mind's awareness of its own operations, like willing, thinking, remembering).
- **Complex Ideas**: Created by the mind's active operations—combining, comparing, or abstracting from simple ideas. Examples might be the concept of "beauty" (mixing ideas of form, color, pleasure) or "justice" (combining moral reasoning and social rules).

Locke also introduced the notion of **primary** and **secondary qualities**:

- **Primary Qualities**: Traits like shape, size, motion, and number, which exist in objects themselves.
- **Secondary Qualities**: Traits like color, taste, and sound, which arise from the interaction between primary qualities and our perceptual apparatus.

This distinction influenced future discussions about perception and reality, suggesting that certain aspects of our sensory experiences exist only in our minds rather than as objective features of the external world.

10.3.4. Personal Identity

Locke initiated a debate on **personal identity** that resonates with psychology today. He argued that personal identity depends on **consciousness**—in particular, the continuity of memory. If a person can remember past experiences, they remain the same "self" over time. This approach was novel, moving away from the idea that identity is purely about having the same soul or substance. Instead, Locke's concept made identity psychological in nature, hinging on memory and self-awareness.

Future philosophers, including Hume, would challenge Locke's memory-based account. But Locke's idea that identity involves mental continuity set a precedent for studying the self as a psychological construct rather than a purely metaphysical entity. Modern psychology still wrestles with how memory, personality, and consciousness shape the sense of self.

10.3.5. Educational and Social Implications

Locke's stress on the mind's malleability informed his treatises on education. He believed that proper upbringing and rational instruction could cultivate virtue and wisdom. This notion contributed to the Enlightenment view that social reforms, better schooling, and moral training might improve society by improving the people in it. Locke's ideas also underpinned liberal political theory, championing individual rights and government by consent—both presupposing that individuals can reason about their interests and moral obligations.

Psychologically, Locke established the environment (in tandem with reflection) as central to mental development, challenging prior assumptions about innate dispositions. Though later research in psychology would find complexities not fully accounted for by a strict blank-slate view, Locke's arguments propelled an enduring conversation about the balance between innate faculties and learned experiences.

10.4. David Hume

10.4.1. Hume's Background and Project

David Hume was a Scottish philosopher, historian, and essayist. Influenced by Locke's empiricism and Berkeley's immaterialism, Hume took a bold step toward **skepticism**, questioning whether humans can truly know the nature of reality through reason or experience. In his main philosophical work, A *Treatise of Human Nature* (1739-1740), Hume attempted to create a "science of man" grounded in observation of how the mind works. He believed that understanding human nature—our passions, beliefs, and perceptions—was the key to grounding all other sciences.

However, Hume found that our "common sense" notions of causation, identity, and substance had weaker empirical footing than many realized. This line of argument triggered significant controversy, as it suggested that reason itself might be less stable than Enlightenment optimists believed. Nonetheless, Hume also wrote widely on ethics, aesthetics, and religion, applying his empiricist lens to each domain.

10.4.2. Impressions and Ideas

Hume refined the empiricist distinction between impressions (the vivid, immediate data of sense experience) and ideas (the faint images of these impressions in thinking and reasoning). For Hume, **impressions** are the lively perceptions we get through sensation or emotional experience, while **ideas** are those same perceptions when we recall or imagine them without the immediate stimulus. Ideas, therefore, are derivative of impressions—they are "copies" or "echoes" of our lively sensory and emotional encounters.

This move made Hume a thoroughgoing empiricist: the mind has no content that did not first appear as an impression. He further argued that all complex ideas ultimately trace back to simple impressions combined or associated in various ways. If an idea can't be broken down into simpler impressions, Hume concluded it might be meaningless or illusory.

10.4.3. Critique of Causation

One of Hume's most famous contributions was his analysis of **causation**. He observed that we never directly perceive a "necessary connection" between cause and effect. We only see sequences: one event followed by another event repeatedly. From this repetition, we form a habit of expecting the second event whenever we see the first. But this expectation is psychological, not a certain logical necessity.

For instance, when we see one billiard ball strike another and the second ball moves, we infer a cause-effect relationship. But Hume argued this inference rests on custom and habit, not on rational certainty that the future must resemble the past. This critique had enormous implications. It suggested that many of our scientific and everyday assumptions about cause and effect rely on induction, which itself cannot be justified purely rationally. Philosophers ever since have wrestled with the so-called "problem of induction," and the question of whether our belief in causality can be proven or only accepted as a practical necessity.

10.4.4. The Self as a Bundle of Perceptions

Hume also challenged Locke's emphasis on memory-based personal identity. He found no single impression of "self" beyond fleeting perceptions—thoughts, sensations, emotions—that succeed each other with great rapidity. Thus, the self might be nothing more than a "bundle" or "heap" of interconnected perceptions, bound by the mind's associative mechanisms rather than by any persistent identity.

This position is often called the "bundle theory" of the self. It destabilized the notion of a continuous ego or soul that endures through time. Hume recognized that people still have a strong sense of personal identity, but he attributed it to the imaginative process that connects our memories and impressions. This radical skepticism about the self foreshadowed modern debates in psychology and neuroscience about whether a stable, unified self truly exists or is instead a constructed narrative.

10.4.5. Emotions and Morality

Hume's analysis of human nature extended to the emotions—what he called "passions." He believed reason is largely the slave of the passions; we act because we feel, and reason mostly helps us figure out how to achieve the ends our feelings dictate. Morality, in Hume's view, arises from sentiments of approval or disapproval. We feel sympathetic pleasure when we see virtuous actions, and we recoil from vice. Hence, moral judgments come from emotions, not from rational deduction.

This approach placed Hume in contrast with rationalist moral philosophers like Kant, who later argued that moral duties stem from reason. In psychological terms, Hume's emphasis on sentiment anticipated modern affective theories of morality, which see moral responses as deeply rooted in emotion or empathy rather than purely rational calculations.

10.5. Comparative Reflections on Descartes, Locke, and Hume

1. **Epistemology**:
    - Descartes believed in innate ideas and deductive certainty.
    - Locke denied innate ideas, seeing the mind as a blank slate shaped by experience.

- Hume took empiricism to its skeptical limits, showing how experiences alone might not guarantee certainty about causality or the self.
2. **Mind-Body and Consciousness**:
    - Descartes introduced dualism and the focus on subjective thought ("I think, therefore I am").
    - Locke was less concerned with mind-body metaphysics; he saw mental operations as reliant on bodily sensations, but did not systematically address how mind and body interact.
    - Hume sidestepped much of the metaphysical debate, emphasizing that even the concept of a stable mind or self is questionable.
3. **Identity and Self**:
    - Descartes anchored identity in the thinking substance (the soul).
    - Locke tied personal identity to memory and continuous consciousness.
    - Hume dissolved the self into a bundle of fleeting perceptions bound by habit.
4. **Moral Psychology**:
    - Descartes did not write extensively about morality within the context of mind.
    - Locke's focus was on moral ideas derived from social experiences and rational reflection.
    - Hume located morality primarily in emotive responses and sympathies, thus focusing on the psychological basis of ethical judgments.
5. **Methodological Influence**:
    - Descartes's methodological doubt established introspection and rational clarity as core philosophical tools.

- Locke's emphasis on experience and observation informed educational reforms and progressive social thought.
- Hume's careful psychological analysis of cause-effect reasoning, personal identity, and moral sentiment set the stage for further skepticism and eventually for scientific approaches that test how humans actually perceive, remember, and reason.

10.6. Long-Term Consequences for Psychology

The works of Descartes, Locke, and Hume significantly shaped the evolution of psychological thought:

- **Rationalism vs. Empiricism**: Their conflicting viewpoints on the sources of knowledge echo through subsequent debates about how to study and understand the mind. Early experimental psychology in the 19th century leaned heavily on empirical methods, but rationalist threads remained in theories emphasizing innate mental structures.
- **Nature vs. Nurture**: Locke's blank-slate notion advanced the idea that nurture and environment are pivotal, whereas Descartes's focus on innate ideas implied a stronger role for nature. Modern psychology still wrestles with how to balance these forces.
- **Scientific Skepticism**: Hume's skepticism underscored that many assumptions (like causation) are mental habits rather than logically provable facts. This perspective encouraged careful scrutiny of how we gather and interpret evidence—a principle fundamental to scientific research.
- **The Self and Consciousness**: The question of whether there is a stable, unifying self or soul resonates in contemporary fields like cognitive science, psychology of personality, and neuroscience. Hume's and Locke's theories on identity still

inform discussions about memory, continuity, and self-concept.

10.7. Conclusion

Descartes, Locke, and Hume stand as three cornerstones of early modern thought on the mind, each promoting a distinct approach:

- **Descartes**: Dualist rationalism with emphasis on innate knowledge and the thinking self.
- **Locke**: Empiricist theory of knowledge, rejecting innate ideas and highlighting the environment's formative power on the mind.
- **Hume**: Skeptical extension of empiricism, challenging the certainty of causation, the permanence of the self, and even the basis of morality in reason.

Their ideas directly seeded many lines of inquiry that would later bloom into philosophical psychology, and eventually into a separate scientific discipline in the 19th century. They also influenced how educators, political theorists, and scientists of their time conceived of human nature, knowledge, and social organization.

As we advance in our historical narrative, we will see how these early modern debates laid a foundation for the eventual transition from purely philosophical speculation to more empirical, laboratory-based studies of sensation, perception, and cognition. In the next chapters, we will examine that transition: how natural philosophy and physiology converged to create the first stirrings of scientific psychology—ultimately leading to formal experimental labs, psychophysics, and the establishment of psychology as a recognized academic field.

CHAPTER 11: TRANSITION TO SCIENTIFIC PSYCHOLOGY

11.1. Introduction

Throughout the late 18th and early 19th centuries, philosophical debates over the nature of mind, knowledge, and behavior continued. Building on Enlightenment ideas, scholars increasingly called for more concrete, systematic methods to study human mental processes. This search for empirical rigor paved the way for **scientific psychology**, a discipline that would move beyond pure speculation to laboratory-based investigation.

In previous chapters, we saw how thinkers like Descartes, Locke, and Hume set the philosophical foundations. By the mid-19th century, other forces encouraged a shift toward experimentation: advancements in **physiology**, **biology**, and **physics** showed that precise measurement of natural phenomena was possible. Scientists like Helmholtz and Weber sought to measure aspects of sensation, revealing that even intangible experiences—like touch or vision—could be quantified to some extent. This melding of philosophy with experimental science laid the crucial groundwork for psychology's eventual recognition as a legitimate scientific field.

This chapter explores the pivotal transition from armchair philosophizing and introspection to systematic experimentation on human perception, reaction times, and mental processes. We will see how intellectual currents, new instruments, and cross-disciplinary collaborations converged, turning "philosophical psychology" into something more empirical. We will also look at influential figures—like Fechner and Helmholtz—who connected the study of the mind with the laws of the physical world, thus helping to forge the path for Wilhelm Wundt's founding of the first psychological laboratory in 1879.

11.2. Key Intellectual Currents in the Early 19th Century

11.2.1. Romanticism's Influence

The late 18th and early 19th centuries saw a flourishing of **Romanticism** in Europe. This cultural and intellectual movement reacted against the Enlightenment's heavy emphasis on reason, championing emotion, individual creativity, and subjective experience. Romantic poets and philosophers insisted that human consciousness possessed qualities not captured by purely mechanistic or rational analyses—emphasizing imagination, intuition, and the mysterious depths of the self.

Though Romanticism itself did not yield a formal scientific approach, it highlighted aspects of the mind that previous rationalist and empiricist philosophies often downplayed. This renewed interest in the complexity of subjective experience ironically supported later experimental psychologists, who recognized that internal experiences—emotions, sensations, volition—deserved systematic investigation. So while Romanticism did not directly give rise to lab experiments, it validated the internal realm as a major focus, paving the way for future attempts to measure and categorize mental events.

11.2.2. The Legacy of Kant and the German Philosophical Scene

Immanuel Kant (1724–1804), whose works we briefly referenced, had a major impact on how German universities approached the study of mind. Kant famously argued that while we can systematically explore phenomena (the appearances shaped by our mental faculties), the "noumenal" realm (things-in-themselves) remains inaccessible. This viewpoint led to some skepticism about whether the mind, in itself, could be studied scientifically in the same manner as physical objects.

Nevertheless, Kant's successors—Fichte, Schelling, and Hegel—further explored consciousness, self, and reason as dynamic processes. Their idealist philosophies made "mind" central to the understanding of reality. Meanwhile, other thinkers, such as Herbart and Lotze, sought to integrate mathematics and systematic methods into psychology, stepping away from purely speculative idealism. These developments in German thought encouraged careful analysis of mental processes, even as debate persisted over whether the mind could be approached with the same empirical rigor as the natural sciences.

11.2.3. Positivism in France

Across the Rhine, French intellectual culture took a different route under the banner of **Positivism**, advanced by Auguste Comte (1798–1857). Positivism held that only knowledge derived from empirical observation and logical reasoning (preferably mathematical) could be considered valid. Comte originally placed psychology in the realm of "metaphysics," doubting its ability to become a true science because thoughts could not be measured directly. However, his framework underscored a broader shift: the sense that real knowledge must be grounded in observable, verifiable data.

This emphasis on observation and measurement, despite Comte's skepticism about psychology, resonated with those who believed the mind might be studied objectively through careful experiments or physiological measurements. Gradually, psychologists—especially in Germany—would show that mental processes could indeed be probed using objective methods, bridging the gap between Comte's positivist criteria and the intangible realm of subjective experience.

11.3. Advances in Physiology

11.3.1. The Rise of Experimental Physiology

By the early 19th century, physiology was emerging as a robust experimental science. Researchers dissected animals, measured nerve conduction, studied the sensory organs, and began mapping out how bodily functions worked. This empirical focus on **how** processes occurred (rather than purely **why** they occurred) marked a shift from older medical traditions to a more scientific approach.

Two factors made this shift possible:

1. **Improved Instruments**: Innovations like more accurate scales, chronometers, and galvanometers allowed scientists to quantify small changes in weight, time, and electrical current, enabling them to measure aspects of the nervous system.
2. **Reductionist Mindset**: Many physiologists believed that understanding smaller components—like nerves and reflex arcs—would reveal how the entire organism functioned, including mental activity.

Through meticulous observation and controlled experiments, these physiologists offered new insights into the biological substrate of the mind. If the function of each sense organ could be mapped, and if neural impulses could be timed, then perhaps the same careful study could be extended to more complex mental operations.

11.3.2. Bell-Magendie Law and the Reflex Arc

An early breakthrough in understanding the nervous system came from the **Bell-Magendie Law**, named after Charles Bell (1774–1842) and François Magendie (1783–1855). Their work distinguished **sensory** (afferent) nerves, which carry information from the senses to the spinal cord, from **motor** (efferent) nerves, which carry commands from the spinal cord to the muscles. Although the details of who discovered what first were contested, the result was clarity: the spinal cord had separate pathways for incoming sensory signals and outgoing motor impulses.

This basic principle informed the concept of a **reflex arc**—the idea that certain actions are automatic responses to specific stimuli, mediated by the spinal cord rather than conscious will. The reflex arc provided a physiological model that could be used to explain fundamental units of behavior. While not psychology in the modern sense, it illuminated how the body handled input and output, giving psychologists a framework for exploring how sensation and reaction might be measured or even timed in the lab.

11.3.3. Localization of Function in the Brain

Another critical line of research involved **localization of function** in the brain. Early attempts, like **phrenology**—pioneered by Franz Joseph Gall (1758–1828)—claimed that bumps on the skull corresponded to personality traits. Though we now consider phrenology a pseudoscience, it represented an attempt to link psychological characteristics to specific brain areas.

More rigorous evidence came from clinical observations, such as those by **Paul Broca (1824–1880)**. Broca identified a region in the left frontal lobe associated with speech production (now called "Broca's area"), after studying a patient who could understand language but not speak. Similar findings by Karl Wernicke (1848–1905) for language comprehension gave further support to the notion that complex mental faculties could be tied to distinct brain regions.

This localization movement indicated a path forward: mental functions were increasingly seen as embodied in physiological structures. As a result, psychologists became more confident that objective, scientific study of the mind was feasible if they could link mental activities to measurable brain processes.

11.4. Pioneers of Psychophysics

11.4.1. Ernst Heinrich Weber: The Just Noticeable Difference

Ernst Heinrich Weber (1795–1878) was a German physician who researched sensory perception, particularly the senses of touch and kinesthesis. He uncovered a phenomenon now known as the **just noticeable difference (JND)**: the smallest detectable change in a stimulus that a person can reliably notice. For instance, if you hold a weight of 50 grams in one hand and 51 grams in the other, you might not detect a difference; but at some threshold—say 55 grams vs. 50 grams—you become aware of it.

Weber systematically varied stimuli (like weights, lengths of lines on the skin, or loudness of tones) and measured the smallest detectable change. From these experiments, he observed that the ratio between the initial stimulus and the increment remained remarkably constant for each sense. This became known as **Weber's Law**:

$$\frac{\Delta I}{I} = k$$

where ΔI is the change in stimulus intensity needed to produce a JND, I is the initial stimulus intensity, and k is a constant specific to each sensory modality. Weber's Law was groundbreaking because it introduced mathematical precision into the study of sensation, showing that subjective sensory experiences could be measured in a quantitative way.

11.4.2. Gustav Theodor Fechner: Linking Mind and Matter

Building on Weber's work, **Gustav Theodor Fechner (1801–1887)** took psychophysics further. Trained in physics, Fechner wanted to reconcile the physical world (measurable stimuli) with mental experience (sensation). In his seminal text, *Elements of Psychophysics* (1860), Fechner proposed a mathematical relationship between the intensity of a physical stimulus and the intensity of the resulting psychological sensation.

Fechner's famous formula, which refined Weber's Law, is often expressed as:

$$S = k \log(I)$$

where S is the subjective sensation, I is the physical stimulus intensity, and k is a constant. This logarithmic relationship suggested that as stimulus intensity grows, the sensation does not increase linearly but slows down. For example, if you double the brightness of a light, you may not perceive it as twice as bright.

Fechner's approach broke new ground because he attempted to quantify the mind-body relationship. He coined the term "psychophysics" to describe this field, bridging subjective experience and objective measurement. While there were debates about the theoretical underpinnings of Fechner's formula, his work established a model for how one might systematically study perception using controlled experiments, paving the way for experimental psychology to flourish.

11.4.3. Hermann von Helmholtz: Speed of Nerve Conduction and Sensation

Hermann von Helmholtz (1821–1894) was a polymath: physician, physicist, and physiologist. Helmholtz's contributions to psychology include:

1. **Measurement of Nerve Conduction Velocity**: Contrary to an earlier assumption that nerve impulses traveled instantaneously, Helmholtz measured the speed of neural

signals in frogs and later in human nerves. He found the speed to be relatively slow (on the order of tens of meters per second), proving neural conduction was a physical process bound by time. This discovery was vital for psychology, revealing that mental events—like perceiving a stimulus or initiating a response—might be measured if one could track the timing of nerve impulses.
2. **Theory of Color Vision**: Helmholtz expanded Thomas Young's trichromatic theory, positing that the human eye has three types of color receptors (roughly corresponding to red, green, and blue). While modern refinements exist, the core idea explained many color vision phenomena. By analyzing how receptors combined signals, Helmholtz's theory demonstrated that complex mental experiences (color perception) could be explained in terms of simpler physiological processes.
3. **Research on Audition**: Helmholtz also investigated the perception of sound, analyzing how the ear decomposes complex sounds into their component frequencies. This contributed to the study of how the mind interprets stimuli from the environment.

Helmholtz's rigorous experimental methods influenced generations of scientists. His commitment to the principle of **conservation of energy** in physiology also reinforced the notion that mental and physical processes followed natural laws. If nerve conduction was measurable and obeyed physical constraints, it suggested a continuity between the mental and the material—an insight further legitimizing the scientific study of the mind.

11.5. Reaction-Time Studies

11.5.1. The Concept of Mental Chronometry

By the mid-19th century, researchers realized they could measure **reaction times** (RTs) to gain insight into the temporal dynamics of mental processes. If the conduction speed of nerves was finite, then the time between a stimulus (e.g., a light flash) and a person's response (e.g., pressing a button) might reflect not just nerve travel time but also the mental steps involved in perceiving, deciding, and initiating movement.

Friedrich Bessel (1784–1846) initially studied reaction times in astronomy to account for the "personal equation": different astronomers recorded star transits at slightly different times. Bessel discovered that each observer had a characteristic reaction delay, leading to the practice of calibrating or correcting for individual differences. Though Bessel was not studying "psychology," his approach—that personal variation in timing was systematic—had clear implications for measuring mental processes.

Later, scientists such as **Cornelis Donders (1818–1889)** in the Netherlands formalized reaction-time methodologies. Donders introduced tasks that required increasingly complex decisions, showing how the differences in RT between tasks could be used to infer the duration of specific mental operations. For example, comparing a simple RT task (press a button when you see a light) to a choice RT task (press one button if the light is green, another if the light is red) revealed the added time required for discrimination and decision-making.

This **subtractive method** allowed experimenters to estimate the duration of distinct mental stages, pushing psychology toward the domain of quantitative experimentation. Though the subtractive method had limitations, it underscored a growing realization: mental activity could be dissected into measurable intervals, bridging the previously abstract realm of "mind" with the measurable realm of "time."

11.5.2. Controversies and Refinements

Reaction-time studies were not without debate. Critics argued that subtracting one RT from another might oversimplify mental processes. If the tasks differed in more than one mental operation, the results could be ambiguous. Additionally, researchers had to assume that mental processes occurred in strictly sequential stages, with no overlap—an assumption that might not always hold.

Nevertheless, the broader point remained: reaction-time experiments demonstrated that mental events required time, that they could be systematically manipulated (by changing task complexity), and that measurements could yield quantitative data about cognition. This was revolutionary compared to centuries of philosophical speculation on the mind. It hinted that the "mental chemistry" approach—where one breaks down complex mental events into simpler components—was viable.

11.6. Shifting Academic Contexts

11.6.1. The German University System

One reason Germany became the cradle of experimental psychology was its university system. In the early 19th century, German universities—reformed under the influence of Wilhelm von Humboldt—encouraged research as a fundamental part of faculty duties. Professors were expected not just to teach established doctrines but to generate new knowledge. They had resources to set up laboratories, conduct experiments, and guide students in original research.

This environment contrasted with some other European nations where universities focused on preserving tradition or training professionals (clergy, lawyers, doctors) without strong emphasis on new empirical inquiry. Thus, when figures like Weber, Fechner, and

Helmholtz presented their findings, they did so within supportive institutional frameworks that valued experimental data and recognized the potential to systematically investigate mental processes.

11.6.2. Philosophical Chairs and the Emergence of Psychology

Throughout German universities, "philosophy" encompassed not just metaphysics and epistemology but also what we now call the natural sciences. Chairs in philosophy often included areas we would see as psychology, logic, or even physiology. Pioneers like Fechner and Wundt came from backgrounds that straddled physics, physiology, and philosophy, allowing them to forge new methods bridging these domains.

Because these scholars held positions in philosophy faculties, the shift toward an empirical study of the mind was partly a redefinition of what "philosophy" could include. By the 1860s and 1870s, it became clearer that the "psychology" portion of philosophy was detaching itself, requiring specific lab apparatus, systematic observation, and experimental designs. This transition set the stage for Wilhelm Wundt to establish the first official laboratory devoted exclusively to psychological research.

11.7. The Global Intellectual Climate

11.7.1. British Empiricist Legacy

While Germany led in laboratory-based methods, the British tradition of empiricism—Locke, Berkeley, Hume—still influenced psychological thought. British thinkers like **Alexander Bain (1818–1903)** combined philosophical psychology with physiology in works like *The Senses and the Intellect* (1855) and *The Emotions and the Will* (1859). Bain explored how bodily states and mental states interacted, describing how habits form and linking them to neural changes. He also helped found the journal *Mind* in 1876, which published early experimental findings alongside philosophical discussions.

John Stuart Mill (1806–1873), another British philosopher, championed a more "scientific" approach to psychology, arguing for a mental chemistry in which complex ideas derived from simpler "mental elements." Although Mill did not run experiments himself, he pushed for the notion that psychology should use inductive, scientific methods akin to the natural sciences. These British developments dovetailed with the German experimental tradition, reinforcing the sense that psychology was becoming an empirical field in multiple regions.

11.7.2. American Intellectual Context

Across the Atlantic, American universities gradually adopted German models, sending promising students to study under German professors. By the 1870s and 1880s, returning Americans brought back the new experimental techniques, helping to establish psychological labs in the United States—most notably at Johns Hopkins University (1883) and later at other institutions. This transatlantic flow of ideas foreshadowed the explosion of psychological research in the U.S. in the early 20th century.

Moreover, American pragmatism, exemplified by Charles Sanders Peirce and William James, provided a philosophical environment open to empirical inquiry and interested in how mental processes function in real life. Though the major developments in American psychology lie beyond the immediate scope of this chapter, it is important to note that the seeds were sown during the same transitional period.

11.8. Implications for the Birth of Experimental Psychology

By the 1870s, the convergence of these trends—physiological measurement, psychophysical laws, reaction-time methods, supportive university environments—placed psychology on the brink of recognition as a distinct scientific discipline. Philosophers no longer had to rely solely on introspective speculation; they had tools, formulas, and apparatus for testing hypotheses about perception, judgment, and cognition.

Important shifts included:

1. **Methodological Innovations**: Psychophysics, reaction-time procedures, and physiological research gave psychologists tangible ways to measure subjective phenomena.
2. **Institutional Support**: German universities in particular nurtured "philosophical" investigations with empirical methods, legitimizing the establishment of labs dedicated to investigating the mind.
3. **Conceptual Frameworks**: With influences from Romantic introspection, Kantian debates on the limits of knowledge, and positivist calls for verifiable data, psychology had a broad theoretical ground.

This prepared the stage for the pivotal moment often marked as the "official" start of scientific psychology: **Wilhelm Wundt's founding of the first psychological laboratory at the University of Leipzig in 1879**. Wundt, building on the legacies of Weber, Fechner, Helmholtz, and others, demonstrated that mental processes were amenable to systematic experimentation. Once a separate lab and journal dedicated to psychological research existed, the discipline began to formalize, attracting students from around the world.

CHAPTER 12: WILHELM WUNDT AND THE FIRST LABORATORIES

12.1. Introduction

One year often cited as the "official" start date for modern psychology is **1879**—the year Wilhelm Wundt (1832–1920) established a laboratory at the University of Leipzig dedicated to psychological research. Though this date is symbolic—building on many earlier developments—Wundt's lab represented a clear institutional recognition of psychology as an experimental science. Over the next decades, this lab attracted students from across Europe and America, who spread Wundt's methods far and wide.

In this chapter, we will explore Wilhelm Wundt's life and intellectual contributions, the nature of his laboratory research, and how his approach shaped the discipline's early goals. We will also discuss how other labs soon followed, fueling a surge of experimental investigations into sensation, perception, attention, and the basic processes of consciousness. Despite some controversies and methodological challenges, Wundt's establishment of a formal program for training "experimental psychologists" laid a crucial cornerstone in psychology's history.

12.2. Wilhelm Wundt's Early Years and Influences

12.2.1. From Medicine to Physiology

Wilhelm Maximilian Wundt was born in 1832 in Baden, Germany. He initially studied medicine at the University of Tübingen, then at Heidelberg, receiving his MD in 1856. Like many intellectuals of his time, Wundt found the intersection of philosophy and physiology compelling. Under the mentorship of **Hermann von Helmholtz** at the University of Heidelberg, Wundt worked as an assistant, pursuing research on physiology and the mechanisms of perception.

During the 1860s, Wundt wrote a textbook on human physiology and taught courses that included topics bridging physiology and psychology. He also published **Contributions to the Theory of Sense Perception (1858–1862)** and later his seminal work **Lectures on Human and Animal Psychology (1863)**, foreshadowing the approach he would systematize in Leipzig. These works demonstrated Wundt's conviction that the mind could be studied experimentally, an idea he expanded upon in a major treatise: *Principles of Physiological Psychology* (*Grundzüge der physiologischen Psychologie*), first published in 1873–1874.

12.2.2. Philosophical Foundations

Although Wundt drew heavily from experimental physiology, he was deeply immersed in the German philosophical tradition, including Kant, Herbart, and others who debated the possibility of a "science of mind." Wundt's stance was that mental phenomena, while distinct from physical phenomena, could still be approached systematically through **introspection**, combined with precise measurement and experimental control.

He disagreed with earlier philosophers who thought the mind was too elusive for quantitative methods. Wundt argued that while we might not measure the soul in a metaphysical sense, we could measure reaction times, thresholds, and other observable indicators of mental processes. This approach established Wundt as a pioneer in bridging philosophical questions about consciousness with experimental rigor.

12.3. The Founding of the Leipzig Laboratory

12.3.1. Official Recognition

In 1875, Wundt accepted a position at the University of Leipzig as a professor of philosophy. Four years later, in **1879**, he established what is often called the first laboratory for experimental psychology. Initially a small room with modest apparatus, it soon grew in both scope and reputation. By **1883**, the Leipzig laboratory gained official university status and a separate budget. This was significant because it meant the university formally acknowledged "psychology" as a distinct experimental field rather than a mere adjunct of philosophy or physiology.

Wundt also founded the journal **Philosophische Studien** in 1881 to publish experimental findings from Leipzig. This journal played a central role in disseminating new methods and results to scholars across Europe, signaling that psychological research had its own dedicated forum, similar to scientific journals in other disciplines.

12.3.2. The Laboratory Setting

Wundt's lab contained devices for measuring reaction times, examining sense discrimination, and analyzing attention and memory processes. Common apparatus included **chronoscopes** (to measure very short time intervals), **kymographs** (which recorded changes over time on rolling drums of paper), **aesthesiometers** (for touch thresholds), and other custom-built instruments.

Students performed carefully designed experiments, often on themselves or each other, controlling variables like stimulus duration, intensity, and the intervals between stimuli. By systematically manipulating and measuring these parameters, Wundt hoped to uncover basic "laws" of mental functioning analogous to how physics derived laws of motion. Even though the data often dealt with subjective phenomena (e.g., how bright a light appears), the measurement aspect imparted objectivity and repeatability to the studies.

12.4. Wundt's Conception of Psychology

12.4.1. The Goal: Analysis of Consciousness

Wundt described his approach as the **analysis of the elements of consciousness**. He believed consciousness could be broken down into immediate experiences—sensations, feelings, and images—that combine to form more complex mental states. Experimental psychology, in his view, should identify these basic mental elements and understand how they are organized via "mental chemistry" or associative processes.

Crucially, Wundt distinguished between **immediate experience** (the direct contents of consciousness, such as the sensation of color or tone) and **mediate experience** (interpretations or conceptualizations of those sensations). Psychology's task was to investigate immediate experiences, seeking to describe their qualities, intensities, and durations through introspective self-reports under controlled conditions.

12.4.2. Introspection Under Control

Although introspection had a long history in philosophy, Wundt attempted to transform it into a rigorous, laboratory-based method. He set strict conditions:

1. Observers (often trained students) had to be thoroughly educated on how to observe their mental states without relying on casual reflection.
2. Stimuli were presented in a controlled manner with precise timing.
3. Observers were required to respond quickly (e.g., by pressing a key) to avoid retrospective contamination by memory or subjective interpretation.
4. Repeated trials established reliability and consistency in observations.

Wundt's experiments might, for example, require an observer to report the timing of a simple sensation, or to distinguish the presence of a faint sound, measuring how changes in stimuli altered the subject's conscious experience. The data included reaction times, thresholds, and verbal self-reports. Wundt believed these structured methods would yield valid insights into how simple mental processes operate, though he acknowledged introspection's limitations when it came to higher mental processes like language, culture, and thought.

12.4.3. Two-Tiered Approach: Experimental and Volkerpsychologie

Wundt recognized that complex mental functions—such as language, social customs, religious beliefs—were not easily studied through lab experiments. Hence, he proposed **Völkerpsychologie** (often translated as "cultural psychology" or "ethnic psychology"), a second branch of psychology dealing with higher processes. He wrote extensively on topics like language, myth, art, and social customs, arguing these domains required historical and comparative methods rather than purely experimental ones.

This two-tiered approach indicated Wundt's broad vision. While experimental psychology was suitable for analyzing immediate experiences (perception, sensation, simple associations), cultural psychology examined the collective creations of human societies, where introspection and controlled experiments were less applicable. Modern psychology has often neglected Wundt's cultural psychology legacy, but it demonstrated his holistic view of the discipline as spanning both individual mental processes and societal phenomena.

12.5. The Spread of Wundt's Influence

12.5.1. Training a Generation of Psychologists

Wundt's Leipzig lab drew students from many countries—Germany, the United States, England, Russia, Japan—eager to learn the new scientific techniques. These students completed dissertations under Wundt, then returned home to found labs of their own, effectively propagating the Leipzig model worldwide. Some notable examples:

- **G. Stanley Hall (1846-1924)**: An American who studied briefly with Wundt, returning to the U.S. to found the first American psychology lab at Johns Hopkins (1883) and later establishing the American Psychological Association (1892).
- **James McKeen Cattell (1860-1944)**: Another American student, who became the first professor of psychology in the U.S. at the University of Pennsylvania and later championed mental testing.
- **Hugo Münsterberg (1863-1916)**: A German student of Wundt who moved to Harvard, contributing to applied fields like forensic and industrial psychology.

- **Oswald Külpe (1862–1915)**: A German student who later led the Würzburg School, exploring higher mental processes with refined introspective methods.

These figures and many others adapted Wundt's methods, sometimes diverging significantly from his original vision. Nonetheless, their global dissemination of experimental psychology practices gave the discipline a truly international character by the early 20th century.

12.5.2. Rival Labs and Institutional Growth

Wundt's success inspired rival labs in Germany, such as those established by **Ebbinghaus** (who studied memory), **Stumpf** (who focused on acoustics and phenomenology of music), and others. The competition spurred methodological refinements and expansions of research topics. Psychology departments began to emerge in universities, offering formal curricula, awarding degrees, and publishing specialized journals.

By the early 1900s, the notion that psychology was an experimental science—one that belonged in the same academic sphere as physics, chemistry, and biology—had become more accepted. Journals like **Mind**, **American Journal of Psychology**, and others published empirical articles. Scientific conferences showcased new findings on sensation, memory, learning, and more.

12.6. Experimental Topics in Early Laboratories

12.6.1. Sensory Thresholds and Psychophysics

Given their heritage from Weber and Fechner, early labs devoted much attention to psychophysics—determining thresholds for detecting stimuli (absolute thresholds) and the smallest noticeable changes (difference thresholds). This research aimed to map out the relationship between physical stimulus intensity and subjective experience, refining Fechner's logarithmic law or testing alternative formulas.

Studies included systematic measurements of brightness, color perception, tonal frequencies, and more. Researchers used specialized instruments like **photometers** for light intensity or **audiometers** for sound levels. These experiments served as the foundation for the broader claim that psychology could produce quantifiable, law-like findings.

12.6.2. Reaction Times and Attention

Wundt's lab continued the tradition of **mental chronometry**, building upon Donders's subtractive method. Researchers devised tasks requiring participants to detect stimuli, discriminate among them, and respond differently based on experimental conditions. By comparing reaction times across tasks, they hoped to infer the durations of distinct mental operations, such as perception, decision-making, or motor initiation.

A related focus was **attention**. Wundt believed attention to be an active process that affects conscious experience. Experiments tried to gauge how quickly attention could shift, how many stimuli could be processed at once, and how dividing attention impacted accuracy and speed. Though these studies might seem rudimentary by modern standards, they introduced systematic ways to investigate a process long considered ineffable.

12.6.3. Association and Memory

Although not as central in Wundt's lab as in Ebbinghaus's later independent work, the Leipzig researchers did investigate simple forms of **association**—how presenting one stimulus might elicit recall of a related idea. They measured the time it took to form associations or to recall words in a list, aiming to quantify memory processes.

Wundt believed that complex memory processes would require more than simple reaction-time tasks. Nonetheless, these early attempts laid the groundwork for understanding how repeated experiences shape mental connections—a stepping stone to more extensive memory research that would soon flourish, including Ebbinghaus's classic studies on nonsense syllables.

12.7. Criticisms and Limitations of Wundt's Approach

12.7.1. Introspection Debates

While Wundt insisted on a controlled form of introspection, critics argued that self-observation is inevitably subjective and prone to bias. Could observers accurately dissect their own moment-to-moment experiences without altering those experiences by the act of observation? **Franz Brentano** and later the Würzburg School (Oswald Külpe) claimed that Wundt's strict introspective protocols missed the essence of mental life, particularly for higher processes like reasoning or imagination.

These disagreements paved the way for new methodologies. Eventually, some psychologists shifted from introspection to studying behavior, marking the advent of the behaviorist revolution in the early 20th century. But in the late 19th century, introspection remained the core method, and Wundt's lab was the leading exponent of how to do it systematically.

12.7.2. Overlooking Applied and Social Aspects

Wundt's lab was primarily concerned with basic mental processes—sensation, perception, reaction times—neglecting more "applied" domains such as clinical conditions or real-world behaviors. Additionally, though Wundt wrote about cultural psychology, he did not integrate it with his experimental program in any systematic way. Observers only rarely tested real-world complexities like language comprehension, social interaction, or motivation inside the lab setting.

This narrow focus caused some to view Wundtian psychology as too academic and detached from practical concerns—an image that, ironically, would later be challenged by American psychologists who pursued practical applications (e.g., educational testing, industrial psychology) at the turn of the 20th century.

12.8. Beyond Leipzig

Wundt's model inspired dozens of similar laboratories in Europe and North America:

- **University of Würzburg** in Germany, led by Külpe, investigated imaginative thought and "mental sets" using variations of introspection.
- **University of Göttingen**, under Georg Elias Müller, contributed extensively to psychophysics, color vision, and memory research.
- **In the United States**, G. Stanley Hall's lab at Johns Hopkins (1883) and later labs at the University of Pennsylvania (James Cattell), Cornell (Edward Titchener, who became Wundt's famous English-language advocate), and other institutions rapidly expanded research in experimental psychology.

By the early 1900s, one could speak of an international community of experimental psychologists. Conferences, journals, and professional associations (like the American Psychological Association, founded in 1892) anchored the new field's institutional presence. Despite variations in emphasis—some labs studied child development, others illusions and sensations—all traced their lineage back to Wundt's foundational approach of controlled experiment and introspective reporting.

12.9. Wundt's Lasting Legacy

1. **Laboratory Methods**: Wundt turned the idea of measuring mental processes into a practical enterprise, establishing protocols and apparatus for systematically collecting data.
2. **Institutional Recognition**: By securing official status for his lab, Wundt demonstrated that psychology could stand alongside other sciences in the university structure.
3. **Training the Next Generation**: Dozens of influential psychologists worldwide began their careers at Leipzig, diffusing Wundt's methods and thereby unifying the emerging discipline's core practices.
4. **Conceptual Foundations**: Wundt's emphasis on dissecting consciousness into elements shaped later movements like **Structuralism** (Edward Titchener) and sparked reactions from **Functionalism**, **Gestalt Psychology**, and eventually **Behaviorism**.
5. **Two-Fold Model of Psychology**: While best known for his lab-based research, Wundt also insisted that higher mental functions (language, culture, social interaction) required different methods—an early forerunner to the idea that certain psychological phenomena are not easily reduced to simple experiments.

CHAPTER 13: STRUCTURALISM AND EDWARD TITCHENER

13.1. Introduction

When Wilhelm Wundt founded the first experimental psychology laboratory in 1879, he offered a systematic approach for investigating the elements of conscious experience. However, the shape of experimental psychology after Wundt took divergent paths. One prominent line of development was **Structuralism**, a school of thought championed most visibly by **Edward Bradford Titchener (1867–1927)**. Structuralism aimed to map the structure of conscious experience by identifying its fundamental components—akin to how chemists might break down complex compounds into basic elements.

Titchener, an Englishman who studied in Germany under Wundt, brought Wundt's approach to the United States. Yet Titchener did not merely replicate Wundt's program; instead, he built his own version of introspective analysis, imposing rules, procedures, and terminologies that became synonymous with Structuralism as practiced in American universities. This chapter explores Titchener's life, his theoretical goals, the methods he promoted, and the debates that surrounded Structuralism before its eventual decline in the early 20th century.

13.2. Edward Bradford Titchener

13.2.1. Early Life in England

Edward Bradford Titchener was born in Chichester, England, in 1867. As a youth, he attended preparatory schools with a strong classical emphasis, showing an aptitude for languages and an inclination toward scholarly pursuits. He subsequently entered Oxford University, studying classics and philosophy. At Oxford, Titchener encountered British empiricist ideas, notably from John Locke and David Hume, which emphasized sensory experience as the foundation of knowledge. These thinkers influenced Titchener's later conviction that complex mental processes arise from simpler sensations or images.

After his undergraduate studies, Titchener developed a strong interest in the new experimental psychology coming out of Germany. He read works by Wilhelm Wundt and Gustav Fechner, persuading him that psychology should be grounded in systematic observation and measurement rather than speculative philosophy alone. Determined to join this emerging scientific field, Titchener decided to travel to Germany for more advanced studies.

13.2.2. Graduate Training Under Wundt

In 1890, Titchener enrolled at the University of Leipzig to study under **Wilhelm Wundt**. Leipzig was by then recognized as the hub of experimental psychology, attracting students worldwide. Titchener spent two years there, immersing himself in Wundt's lab-based approach: measuring reaction times, establishing sensory thresholds, and using meticulously controlled introspection to record immediate experiences.

Titchener's dissertation (completed in 1892) was supervised by Wundt, and it focused on psychophysical measurements. Although Titchener admired Wundt's emphasis on experimental control, he gradually formed his own perspective on how best to dissect consciousness. He felt that Wundt's interests were too broad—especially Wundt's later foray into Völkerpsychologie—and that psychology should remain focused on analyzing conscious experience in precise terms. By the time Titchener returned to

England briefly and then moved on to a career in the United States, he had begun molding the approach that would soon be labeled Structuralism.

13.2.3. Move to the United States and Cornell University

In 1892, Titchener accepted a position at **Cornell University** in Ithaca, New York. Cornell was a prominent American institution, yet it lacked a dedicated program for experimental psychology. Titchener, then only 25, was granted the opportunity to build a laboratory and shape its curriculum as he saw fit. Over the next several decades, he became one of the most influential psychologists in the country, training hundreds of students in his rigorous introspective methods.

At Cornell, Titchener established an environment reminiscent of Leipzig but adapted to American academic structures. He stressed original research by graduate students, careful instruction in introspection, and the use of specialized equipment to measure mental processes. Titchener also published manuals and guides that systematized procedures for introspective experiments, making them accessible to instructors at other universities. His lab at Cornell eventually became the focal point for Structuralist psychology in the United States.

13.3. The Core Principles of Structuralism

13.3.1. The Goal: Identify the Basic Elements of Consciousness

Structuralists believed that the mind, like any complex system, could be understood by breaking it down into its simplest, irreducible components. Titchener argued that just as chemistry advanced by identifying chemical elements and how they combine, psychology would advance by identifying mental elements—such as sensations, images, and affective states—and determining how these elements combined to form more complex mental experiences.

He proposed three broad classes of mental elements:

1. **Sensations**: Basic perceptual experiences (e.g., color, sound, taste) that arise from stimulation of the senses.
2. **Images**: The "pictures" we form in the mind without direct external stimulation, often linked to memory or imagination.
3. **Affective States**: Feelings, such as pleasantness or unpleasantness, that accompany certain experiences.

According to Titchener, every conscious experience at any given moment could be described by specifying (a) which sensations or images were present and (b) the accompanying affective tone. By cataloging and analyzing these elements under controlled conditions, Structuralists hoped to map the architecture of the mind much as a biologist might map the structure of a cell.

13.3.2. Methods: Introspection as the Prime Tool

The hallmark of Structuralism was **introspection**—a systematic process in which trained observers reported the contents of their consciousness. Unlike casual self-observation, Titchener's introspection demanded:

- **Training**: Observers underwent extensive exercises to minimize biases and to report experiences "raw," without interpreting them in everyday language.
- **Immediate Focus**: Observers were instructed to avoid naming or classifying objects (e.g., calling something "a blue circle"). Instead, they might describe the sensation as "a hue of blue with a certain saturation and brightness in a circular field."
- **Avoiding Stimulus Error**: Titchener cautioned against the "stimulus error," which occurred if observers labeled the object rather than describing the immediate sensation. For instance, if shown a piece of fruit, the correct introspective

response would not be "It's an apple." Instead, it should be a list of the color, shape, and possibly an affective feeling.
- **Replicability**: Multiple observers repeated the same tasks under identical conditions to confirm that reported sensations were consistent.

Titchener believed that by stripping away the everyday use of language and focusing on pure sensation, the introspector could reveal the fundamental mental elements underlying conscious experience. This emphasis on methodical, highly trained introspection set Structuralism apart from other emerging approaches that were less reliant on self-report or more interested in function rather than content.

13.3.3. Descriptive Rather Than Interpretive

Structuralism sought to **describe** mental experience, not to explain why it occurred or how it might be used in practical settings. Titchener insisted that psychological science, in its early stages, must focus on describing the "is" rather than investigating the "why" or "how." He believed explanation and application would be premature without a thorough "map" of mental contents.

This descriptive focus separated Titchener's approach from other lines of inquiry that asked, "What is the purpose of consciousness?" or "How does consciousness help an organism adapt?" For Titchener, those questions were secondary until one first cataloged the building blocks of mental life. Structuralism thus took a strongly reductionist stance, aiming to reduce all mental processes to a finite set of basic components.

13.4. Titchener's Laboratory and Research

13.4.1. Experimental Procedures at Cornell

At Cornell, Titchener and his graduate students conducted a wide range of introspective experiments. These often involved:

- **Sensory Discrimination**: Presenting stimuli that varied slightly in brightness, color, or pitch, then asking observers to report the immediate qualities they perceived.
- **Reaction-Time Tasks**: Timing how quickly participants could detect or identify specific sensations, albeit with a structuralist twist: Titchener's interest lay in how participants described the subjective feel of the process, not merely how long it took.
- **Analyses of Feelings**: Attempting to classify affective states into dimensions of pleasantness vs. unpleasantness, excitement vs. calm, and so forth. The lab used various stimuli—like tastes, sounds, or even mild electric shocks—to see how participants described their affective experiences.
- **Studies of Imagery**: Titchener was curious about how individuals formed mental images of objects no longer present. Observers might be asked to recall a visual scene or a piece of music, then introspect about the clarity, vividness, and affective tone of the mental image.

Titchener kept detailed records of these experiments and published both in academic journals and in widely used manuals. The manuals showed instructors how to replicate experiments with introspection, including setting up apparatus, training participants, and analyzing data. In this way, Titchener hoped to standardize introspective methods across various institutions, creating a unified structuralist research program.

13.4.2. The Titchener Manuals

Titchener wrote **Experimental Psychology: A Manual of Laboratory Practice** in multiple volumes, covering qualitative and quantitative experiments. These manuals provided:

1. **Step-by-Step Procedures**: Each experiment described how to set up materials, present stimuli, manage timing, and record observations.
2. **Guidelines for Observer Training**: Titchener outlined how to teach participants to avoid the stimulus error, giving examples of correct and incorrect introspective reports.
3. **Suggested Analyses**: After an experiment, Titchener offered ways to categorize the results into tables reflecting sensation types, intensities, durations, and affective qualities.

The goal was to enable psychology instructors everywhere to adopt structuralist methods, ensuring consistency in how introspective data were gathered. Titchener believed that if enough labs replicated each other's findings, a robust consensus on mental elements would emerge.

13.5. Debates and Criticisms

13.5.1. The Questionable Reliability of Introspection

Almost from the start, Structuralists faced criticism regarding whether introspection could truly yield an objective, reliable account of mental processes. Detractors pointed out that observers might unconsciously interpret their experiences, that repeated practice could alter the nature of the experience itself, or that people simply lacked the capacity to perceive "pure" sensations free from context.

Some psychologists, such as **Oswald Külpe** at the University of Würzburg, found evidence for mental processes that participants could not introspect on easily—"imageless thought," for instance, where people could solve a problem without reporting any distinct images. These findings implied that Titchener's introspection might be missing entire categories of mental activity, especially in more complex cognitive tasks.

13.5.2. Overemphasis on "Elements"

Structuralists were accused of taking a reductionist stance too far, ignoring how the mind functioned in real-world contexts. Critics argued that while analyzing a color patch or a faint sound might be instructive, it told us little about how organisms adapt, learn, or solve problems in everyday life.

A rival school of thought—**Functionalism**—emerged in the United States, championed by figures like William James and John Dewey. Functionalists believed that focusing only on the static elements of consciousness was incomplete. Instead, they asked how consciousness aids survival, how it helps people make decisions, and how it changes in different contexts. Structuralism's narrow focus on dissecting mental contents was thus seen by functionalists as missing the bigger picture of mental life.

13.5.3. The "Stimulus Error" vs. Normal Perception

Titchener's insistence on avoiding the "stimulus error" often felt artificial. In everyday life, people identify objects, not just hues or tones. Telling an observer to call a red apple "a patch of color with a certain brightness and shape" might be instructive in a lab, but some critics claimed it removed essential meaning from perception. They argued that normal perception is inherently interpretive, so trying to strip away all interpretation might yield data that are no longer relevant to ordinary mental processes.

Moreover, participants sometimes found it difficult to adhere to Titchener's rules, slipping into everyday language or simply stating "apple." Titchener would insist such statements be discarded as invalid. This rigid methodology sparked debate over whether psychology should reflect natural cognition or artificially isolate fragments of experience.

13.6. Titchener's Influence on American Psychology

13.6.1. Formation of the "Experimentalists"

To foster discussion among experimental psychologists, Titchener created a group called the **"Experimentalists"** (founded in 1904). It was an informal society that met annually, aiming to provide a forum for researchers to share data, replicate each other's experiments, and refine introspective methods. Titchener personally chose participants, favoring those who aligned with his structuralist orientation. This exclusivity drew some criticism, but the Experimentalists functioned as a hub for scientific discourse, somewhat akin to Wundt's earlier circle in Leipzig.

Curiously, Titchener initially excluded women from the Experimentalists, believing that the frank debates and smoking sessions were not suitable for them. Over time, there was some pushback against this stance. Titchener eventually admitted a few women psychologists, but his original exclusion reflected a broader issue of sexism in early academic psychology. Nevertheless, Titchener did mentor several female graduate students at Cornell, including Margaret Floy Washburn, who became the first woman to earn a Ph.D. in psychology under his direction (though she technically received it while Titchener was at Cornell, the official awarding process also involved the university's acceptance).

13.6.2. Manuals and Pedagogy

Titchener's published manuals had a major impact on how psychology was taught in American colleges. Instructors looking to introduce laboratory exercises found a ready-made curriculum in Titchener's volumes. These labs familiarized students with the notion that psychology could be a hands-on, data-driven field, a significant step in establishing psychology as a mainstream academic discipline.

Though Titchener's brand of Structuralism eventually waned, the idea of lab-based, systematic methodology remained. Future psychologists would adopt and adapt Titchener's teaching approach, even as they challenged his theoretical assumptions. Hence, Titchener inadvertently propelled the institutionalization of psychology in the United States, creating a foundation that more eclectic or functionally oriented psychologists could build upon.

13.7. Decline of Structuralism

By the 1910s and 1920s, Structuralism faced mounting challenges from several directions:

1. **Functionalism**: Focused on mental processes' adaptive functions rather than their elements.
2. **Behaviorism**: Emphasized observable behavior and rejected introspection as too subjective.
3. **Gestalt Psychology**: Argued that consciousness should be studied as whole, integrated patterns rather than sums of parts.
4. **Psychoanalysis**: Proposed a large realm of unconscious mental processes, undermining the idea that consciousness was the primary subject matter.

As these movements gained traction, Titchener's strict introspective method seemed increasingly limited. His lab's concentration on minute sensory distinctions appeared detached from real-world concerns about learning, development, abnormal behavior, or broader cognitive processes. Moreover, younger psychologists found Titchener's tight control over introspection stifling, and they questioned the reliability of data that could not be verified except by trained introspectors.

Titchener continued to refine and defend his system up to his death in 1927, but by then, the professional landscape had shifted. Structuralism was overshadowed by Behaviorism in the United States, which gained enormous influence in the 1920s and 1930s by rejecting introspection outright and focusing on observable stimuli and responses. Despite Titchener's efforts, the mainstream soon moved away from elemental analysis of consciousness.

13.8. Lasting Contributions and Assessments

Although Structuralism did not remain a dominant force, it contributed several lasting impacts:

1. **Methodological Rigor**: Titchener tried to standardize procedures and keep laboratory conditions tightly controlled, helping establish psychology's credibility as an experimental science.
2. **Vocabulary and Concepts**: Terms like "introspection," "stimulus error," and "mental elements" entered psychological discourse, shaping how future researchers discussed the contents of consciousness—even when they eventually critiqued them.
3. **Curricular Influence**: Titchener's manuals and teaching methods popularized laboratory instruction in psychology departments across the United States, which remains a cornerstone of psychological education today.

4. **Female Mentorship**: Despite Titchener's initial exclusion of women from his Experimentalists, he trained several women at Cornell who went on to have significant academic careers, indicating that Structuralism, at least within Titchener's lab, was somewhat more open to female students compared to some other corners of academia at the time.

In retrospect, many psychologists find Titchener's unwavering faith in introspection too restrictive. However, the Structuralist drive to identify fundamental sensations or experiences laid the groundwork for other schools—whether they adopted, adapted, or rejected his approach. Titchener's vision of psychology as a specialized lab science advanced the discipline's reputation, ensuring that university departments allocated resources and recognized the importance of empirical methods.

CHAPTER 14: WILLIAM JAMES AND FUNCTIONALISM

14.1. Introduction

While Edward Titchener in the United States advanced Structuralism by dissecting conscious experience, another prominent figure—**William James (1842–1910)**—proposed a markedly different path for psychology. James's orientation, often labeled **Functionalism**, centered on understanding the **functions** of consciousness and behavior: how mental processes aid individuals in adapting to their environments.

Inspired by Darwin's evolutionary theory and shaped by broad philosophical interests, James saw consciousness not as a static collection of elements but as a continuous "stream" integral to survival and action. Although James disliked strict labels and did not systematically establish "Functionalism" as a formal school, his ideas and teaching strongly influenced a generation of American psychologists. By the early 20th century, Functionalism became a significant rival to Structuralism, paving the way for more applied and pragmatic research programs in psychology.

14.2. William James

14.2.1. Early Life and Varied Interests

William James was born in New York City into an intellectually prominent family—his father, Henry James Sr., was a theologian and philosopher, and his brother, Henry James Jr., became a renowned novelist. William's upbringing involved travel, exposure to diverse cultures, and private tutoring that encouraged independent thinking. As a young man, James pursued art, then switched to chemistry, and finally studied medicine at Harvard Medical School.

During his studies, James developed an interest in philosophy and psychology, partly influenced by reading the works of European scholars. However, personal health issues and existential doubts often interrupted his pursuits. He traveled to Germany in the late 1860s, encountering ideas from the new psychology emerging in Leipzig and other centers. While James respected the experimental methods of Wundt, he was also drawn to broader philosophical questions about free will, faith, and the nature of human experience.

14.2.2. Harvard and the Teaching of Psychology

In 1872, Charles W. Eliot—then the president of Harvard—appointed James as an instructor in physiology. Over time, James's lectures expanded to include topics in psychology and philosophy, leading him to set up a small demonstration lab (though not nearly as extensive as Wundt's or Titchener's) to illustrate psychological principles to students.

James was not as invested in laboratory experimentation as Titchener. Instead, he integrated introspection, personal reflection, examples from literature, and physiological knowledge into a wide-ranging perspective on mental life. By the mid-1880s, James had begun writing what would become his magnum opus—*The Principles of Psychology*, published in 1890. This massive two-volume work laid out James's vision and became a cornerstone for what would evolve into Functionalism.

14.3. The Principles of Psychology and Key Concepts

14.3.1. Stream of Consciousness

One of James's most famous ideas is the **"stream of consciousness."** He argued that consciousness is not a series of separate, static "elements" (as Structuralists suggested) but rather a flowing, continuous process that changes from moment to moment. James compared consciousness to a river or stream, emphasizing its fluidity and unity.

He maintained that trying to dissect consciousness into discrete parts could distort its naturally dynamic character. Each conscious state blends into the next, forming a pattern of thought, perception, and feeling unique to the individual. This concept contrasted sharply with Titchener's methodology, which demanded participants isolate sensation "elements." James believed such isolation was artificial and risked missing how consciousness operates in real life.

14.3.2. Consciousness as Personal and Selective

James stressed that consciousness is **personal**—it belongs to an individual with a particular history, set of experiences, and personality. Moreover, consciousness is **selective**: out of the vast array of stimuli bombarding the senses, people choose (often unconsciously) what to focus on. This selectivity underscores attention as a crucial aspect of mental life.

According to James, we do not passively record reality but actively shape our perception by choosing what to notice, ignore, or emphasize. This selective property of consciousness ties closely to the idea that mental processes have **functions**. By filtering and highlighting relevant information, consciousness serves to guide behavior effectively in a complex environment.

14.3.3. Pragmatism and the Theory of Truth

Though not purely a psychological doctrine, James's **Pragmatism** influenced how he viewed psychological concepts. Pragmatism holds that the truth of an idea depends on its practical consequences—how it helps us navigate the world. James applied this to mental processes: a thought or belief should be evaluated by whether it aids adaptation, not just whether it can be broken into elements.

Hence, consciousness was valuable primarily because it facilitated problem-solving, decision-making, and personal growth. If a concept or mental act "worked" to help an organism function better, that was a mark of its significance. This pragmatic orientation would come to dominate much of early American psychology, shifting the focus to what mental processes do rather than on enumerating their static components.

14.3.4. James-Lange Theory of Emotion

One specific contribution from James to psychology was the **James-Lange theory of emotion** (developed independently by William James and the Danish physiologist Carl Lange). This theory proposed that physiological changes occur first, and then we interpret these changes as emotions. For example, we do not tremble because we are afraid; rather, we feel fear because we become aware of our trembling and other bodily reactions.

While the James-Lange theory was later refined and critiqued, it exemplified James's approach to tying mental processes closely to biological functions. Emotions, he argued, have adaptive value in preparing the organism for action. Studying these physiological-emotional links could illuminate why consciousness includes certain feelings and how those feelings guide behavior.

14.4. Emergence of Functionalism as a Movement

14.4.1. Influence of Evolutionary Theory

One reason Functionalism took root in the United States was the pervasive influence of **Charles Darwin's** theory of evolution by natural selection (published in *On the Origin of Species* in 1859). Darwin's ideas suggested that species developed traits to help them survive and reproduce in specific environments. Many American intellectuals extrapolated from Darwin's biology to human psychology, reasoning that mental processes likely evolved to solve problems and aid adaptation.

Thus, **Functionalism** built on Darwinian logic: if consciousness exists, it should have a purpose—helping the organism respond to challenges, seize opportunities, and maintain well-being. William James embraced this view, arguing that the mind's role should be understood in terms of its utility. Learning, memory, attention, and even emotion all serve vital functions in an individual's interaction with the world.

14.4.2. Functionalist Psychologists at Chicago and Columbia

While James was at Harvard, other psychologists who shared his functional orientation established influential programs elsewhere, notably at:

- **The University of Chicago**: John Dewey, James Rowland Angell, and Harvey Carr advanced a "Chicago School" of Functionalism, studying how mental processes operate in everyday contexts—learning, problem-solving, and adaptation. Dewey's famous 1896 article on the "Reflex Arc Concept in

Psychology" criticized reducing reflexes to simple sensory and motor elements, emphasizing the whole, integrated act.

- **Columbia University**: James McKeen Cattell, influenced by James, Wundt, and Francis Galton, developed mental testing and individual differences research, reflecting a functionalist emphasis on measuring how mind and behavior vary across people in ways that might reflect adaptive functions.

These psychologists cultivated a broad approach: they combined lab experiments with observation, field studies, and a willingness to investigate complex topics like child development, education, or the mental processes underlying problem-solving. This breadth contrasted with Structuralism's narrower focus on adult consciousness in the laboratory.

14.4.3. Divergence from Titchener's Structuralism

Many functionalists criticized Titchener's structural analysis as too narrow and lacking real-world significance. Where Titchener asked, "What are the elements of consciousness, and how do they combine?" functionalists asked, "How does consciousness help an organism survive and flourish?" or "How do learning and memory processes enable effective adaptation?"

Functionalists also gave more attention to **variations among individuals**. In the evolutionary perspective, differences in mental capacity or behavior might reflect different evolutionary pressures or environmental conditions. By studying how people adapt, functionalists believed psychology could illuminate education, mental health, work efficiency, and even social policies.

14.5. James's Students and Their Impact

14.5.1. Mary Whiton Calkins

One of William James's notable students was **Mary Whiton Calkins (1863–1930)**. Despite facing gender-based restrictions, Calkins studied under James at Harvard (though Harvard refused to award her a Ph.D.). She developed the paired-associate method for studying memory, a procedure that paired stimuli (such as numbers) with specific words. Then she measured recall for these pairs, showing how frequency, recency, and vividness influenced memory.

Calkins also proposed a theory of "self-psychology" focusing on the conscious self as the primary subject matter of psychology. Her emphasis on personal identity and subjective experience aligned with James's view that consciousness is personal. Calkins eventually became the first female president of the American Psychological Association (APA) in 1905.

14.5.2. G. Stanley Hall

While not strictly a student of James, **Granville Stanley Hall (1846–1924)** was strongly influenced by James's broader vision of psychology. Hall earned the first American Ph.D. in psychology under James's mentorship (though official awarding processes were complicated), and he later founded the first psychology laboratory in the United States at Johns Hopkins (1883). Hall's interests ranged widely: child psychology, educational reform, adolescence, and even the study of aging.

Inspired by evolutionary ideas, Hall believed studying children's development could reveal "phylogenetic recapitulation"—the notion that child development retraces the evolutionary history of the species. While modern psychology questions this recapitulation idea,

Hall's approach exemplified how Functionalist thinking took Darwinian perspectives seriously. He also established the APA in 1892, demonstrating how functional-minded scholars were building robust institutions for the new discipline.

14.5.3. Other Figures

Several other psychologists who could be broadly termed "functionalist" emerged in this era:

- **James Rowland Angell**: Authored influential texts that defined consciousness in terms of its adaptive significance. As a president of the APA, Angell championed the idea that psychology should address how mental activities function in adjusting to the environment.

- **John Dewey**: Extended Functionalism to educational theory, arguing that schools should foster problem-solving and reflection, mirroring real-world adaptation processes. Dewey's emphasis on "learning by doing" left a major mark on pedagogy.

These individuals carried James's flexible, pragmatic spirit into diverse areas, reinforcing the sense that psychology could address practical questions about learning, mental health, and social well-being.

14.6. The Scope of Functionalist Research

14.6.1. Child Psychology and Educational Applications

Functionalists believed in studying **development** to understand how cognitive processes emerged and changed. This contrasted with Structuralists, who rarely worked with children, focusing instead on trained adult introspectors. Functionalist psychologists observed children in classrooms, collected data on their learning processes, and designed educational experiments.

In line with James's pragmatic outlook, they asked, "How can knowledge of child cognition improve teaching methods?" or "Which types of exercises foster better memory retention?" This question-driven approach paved the way for applied psychology in educational settings, an area that became increasingly influential in the 20th century.

14.6.2. Individual Differences and Mental Testing

Functionalists were also more open to **mental testing** than Titchener. James McKeen Cattell, for instance, introduced measures of reaction time, sensory acuity, and other abilities in an attempt to quantify individual differences. Although these early tests were crude by modern standards, they set the stage for intelligence testing and personality assessment in the decades to follow.

Such an interest in individual variation dovetailed with Darwinian thinking: if mental processes evolved, then people might differ in their inherited capacities or adaptational strategies. Studying these differences could reveal how cognition relates to environment and heredity, shedding light on real-world outcomes—academic achievement, vocational success, or mental health.

14.6.3. Animal Research and Comparative Psychology

Where Titchener's introspection required human verbal reports, functionalists were more willing to investigate **non-human animals** to infer the purposes of behavior. The logic was evolutionary: if humans and other animals share ancestors, then studying how animals learn or perceive might shed light on fundamental adaptive functions of behavior.

Figures like Edward L. Thorndike (though typically classified under "early Behaviorism" or "connectionism") were influenced by functionalist ideas, focusing on how animals solve problems (e.g., puzzle boxes) to glean insights into learning processes that might also operate in humans. James himself famously recounted an anecdote about his own emotions toward a pet dog, illustrating the belief that emotional processes might have parallels in animals and humans.

14.7. Critiques and Tensions

Despite its broad scope, Functionalism encountered certain criticisms:

1. **Lack of Precise Methodology**: Structuralists complained that functionalists sometimes lacked a clear, systematic method akin to introspective analysis. They adopted multiple approaches—observation, questionnaires, mental tests—without a unifying protocol for data collection.

2. **Vague Definition of "Function"**: Critics argued that "function" could mean many things—adapting to environment, guiding behavior, or survival advantage. Some feared that the concept of function was so broad it risked becoming meaningless or failing to generate specific testable hypotheses.

3. **Possible Overreach**: Because functionalists ventured into education, mental health, child development, and social policy, skeptics questioned whether they were conflating science with application, risking the objectivity of their findings in pursuit of practical ends.

Nonetheless, by the first decade of the 20th century, Functionalism was quite influential in American psychology, overshadowing Titchener's Structuralism in many major universities. Its open-ended, eclectic style allowed it to absorb new findings, adopt new methods, and address questions that resonated with public interest—education, child welfare, and mental health—thus strengthening the field's stature.

14.8. William James's Later Life and Legacy

14.8.1. Move Toward Philosophy

After publishing *The Principles of Psychology*, James gradually shifted away from experimental work to focus on broader philosophical and religious questions. He wrote books like *The Will to Believe* (1897) and *The Varieties of Religious Experience* (1902). In these works, James explored faith, mysticism, and personal transformation, always from a pragmatic viewpoint that emphasized the experiential and adaptive dimensions of belief.

Though these writings were more philosophical and less empirical, they remained consistent with James's functional outlook: what matters is how beliefs operate in human life. He maintained correspondence and conversations with philosophers such as Charles Peirce and John Dewey, solidifying Pragmatism as a major American philosophical movement.

14.8.2. Influence on Future Psychology

James's influence spread widely. Even schools that diverged from Functionalism—like Behaviorism—indirectly drew on the idea that psychology should handle real behavior, adaptation, and measurable outcomes. Behaviorists might have rejected the concept of a "stream of consciousness," yet they embraced the functionalist principle that we should study how organisms adjust to their environments.

Beyond academia, James's pragmatic approach resonated with the American public, aligning with cultural values of innovation, practicality, and individual freedom. His lectures and essays gained a broad readership, helping legitimize psychology as a field that could address fundamental human concerns—meaning, motivation, growth—rather than limiting itself to narrow introspective tasks.

14.9. Broader Consequences of Functionalism

1. **Diverse Research Topics**: Functionalism opened the door to studying almost any aspect of human (and animal) behavior and cognition. Child development, mental testing, educational psychology, abnormal behavior—none were off-limits.

2. **Applied Psychology**: Because of its adaptive focus, Functionalism naturally lent itself to practical application. Psychologists researched how to improve learning in schools, how to enhance workplace efficiency, and how to address mental health issues.

3. **Foundation for Future Movements**: Although Behaviorism explicitly rejected introspection and mentalistic terminology, it inherited from Functionalism the drive to study real-world functioning and adaptive behavior. Later, in the mid-20th century, the Cognitive Revolution would also echo some functionalist themes by examining the mind as an active processor of information, again focusing on how mental processes enable effective interaction with the environment.

By the 1910s and 1920s, formal "Functionalism" gave way to various specialized subfields, but the impetus to understand **why** the mind works as it does remained. In that sense, James's perspective never truly disappeared; it was absorbed and transformed as psychology branched out into more specialized areas.

14.10. Comparison

- **Focus**: Structuralists sought the components (sensations, images, affections) of conscious experience; Functionalists examined the purposes of mental processes in adapting to life's demands.

- **Method**: Structuralism relied heavily on trained introspection, trying to minimize interpretive judgments. Functionalism embraced a variety of methods—introspection, observation, tests, and in some cases physiological measures.

- **Scope**: Structuralism confined itself mostly to adult normal consciousness in a lab setting. Functionalism addressed children, animals, individual differences, abnormal behavior, education, and more.

- **Ultimate Goal**: Structuralists wanted an elemental "periodic table" of the mind. Functionalists sought to explain how mind and behavior function in real-time adaptation, often referencing evolutionary theory.

Over time, Functionalism's breadth and practical relevance made it more appealing to a broad base of psychologists, especially in the United States, which was experiencing rapid social and industrial changes that demanded real-world solutions.

CHAPTER 15: PSYCHOANALYSIS

15.1. Introduction

By the late 19th century, experimental psychology had taken root in academic labs, focusing on conscious processes such as perception, memory, and learning. Meanwhile, a radical new perspective emerged in clinical and cultural spheres, eventually challenging the assumption that conscious awareness was the primary seat of the mind. This movement became known as **Psychoanalysis**, founded by **Sigmund Freud (1856–1939)**.

Psychoanalysis proposed that a significant portion of mental life operates below the level of conscious awareness, influencing behavior, emotions, and even physical symptoms. Over time, Freud's ideas attracted devoted followers and also sparked bitter controversies. Two early disciples—**Carl Gustav Jung (1875–1961)** and **Alfred Adler (1870–1937)**—eventually broke with Freud to develop their own schools of "depth psychology." This chapter traces the origins of psychoanalysis, examines Freud's core concepts, and then explores the key divergences brought forth by Jung and Adler.

Although psychoanalysis first gained traction in Vienna and spread primarily through clinical practice, it dramatically influenced broader intellectual thought. It redefined views on childhood development, sexuality, dreams, and the nature of selfhood. By making the **unconscious** central, psychoanalysis challenged the narrower focus on conscious processes that characterized mainstream experimental psychology. Through the 20th century, psychoanalysis significantly impacted literature, art, and popular culture—even as it faced criticism from some scientific psychologists who doubted its methods or empirical foundations.

15.2. The Roots of Psychoanalysis

15.2.1. European Medical Context

During Freud's formative years, the medical community in Europe grappled with disorders that seemed partly mental rather than purely neurological. Patients presented with "hysterical" symptoms—paralyses, sensory losses, fainting spells, or uncontrollable anxieties—that lacked obvious physiological causes. Some physicians, such as Jean-Martin Charcot in Paris, hypothesized that these symptoms could stem from psychological factors, discoverable through techniques like **hypnosis**.

In the late 19th century, Charcot and Hippolyte Bernheim studied hysteria and suggestibility, demonstrating that under hypnosis, patients might recall traumatic experiences or temporarily lose or gain function in a seemingly "suggested" manner. Freud, trained as a physician with a specialty in neurology, became fascinated by these anomalies. He concluded that purely physiological explanations were inadequate, suspecting unconscious mental processes could cause or alleviate hysterical symptoms.

15.2.2. Josef Breuer and the "Talking Cure"

Freud's breakthrough came through collaboration with **Josef Breuer (1842–1925)**, another Viennese physician who treated a famous patient, "Anna O." (real name Bertha Pappenheim). Anna O. suffered from severe physical symptoms and dissociative states. Breuer found that encouraging Anna O. to talk freely about her memories and emotions sometimes relieved her symptoms—a process Anna O. dubbed the "talking cure."

Freud recognized a mechanism in which repressed memories or conflicts emerged when a patient spoke openly, leading to catharsis and partial remission of symptoms. In **Studies on Hysteria** (1895), co-authored by Freud and Breuer, they proposed that hysterical symptoms often stemmed from traumatic memories that had been banished from conscious thought but persisted unconsciously, expressing themselves through somatic or emotional distress.

While Breuer parted ways with Freud over certain theoretical points, this early work laid the foundation for psychoanalysis as a distinct clinical method: using discussion, guided association, and interpretations of hidden conflicts to uncover repressed material and thereby reduce symptoms.

15.3. Sigmund Freud's Core Theories

15.3.1. Topographical and Structural Models of the Mind

Freud introduced different models to describe mental functioning:

1. **Topographical Model**: Divides the mind into three regions:
   - **Conscious**: Thoughts and perceptions within immediate awareness.
   - **Preconscious**: Memories or information that can be brought to consciousness with relative ease.
   - **Unconscious**: Primitive wishes, fears, traumas, and impulses repressed from conscious awareness.
2. Freud believed the unconscious exerted a powerful influence over feelings and behavior, often in disguised or symbolic forms.
3. **Structural Model**: Over time, Freud refined his theory to describe the psyche in terms of three agencies:
   - **Id**: The unconscious reservoir of instinctual drives, seeking immediate gratification (the pleasure principle).

- **Ego**: The rational mediator operating according to the reality principle, trying to balance the id's desires with external demands and social norms.
- **Superego**: The internalized moral standards and ideals, often originating from parental and societal values, which judge and limit the id and ego.

Though Freud's structural model emerged later in his career, it came to define classic psychoanalytic thinking. Conflicts among id, ego, and superego generate much of the emotional turmoil or defense mechanisms seen in everyday life and psychopathology.

15.3.2. Psychosexual Stages

A significant (and controversial) aspect of Freud's theory is his view that personality development proceeds through a series of **psychosexual stages**:

1. **Oral Stage (0–18 months)**: Pleasure centers on the mouth—sucking, biting. Dependence, trust, and comfort are formed (or frustrated) here.
2. **Anal Stage (18–36 months)**: Focus on bowel and bladder elimination, with issues of control and autonomy.
3. **Phallic Stage (3–6 years)**: Children become aware of their genitals, culminating in the Oedipus/Electra complex (a child's unconscious desire for the opposite-sex parent and rivalry with the same-sex parent).
4. **Latency Stage (6–puberty)**: Sexual interests are subdued; children focus on social and intellectual development.
5. **Genital Stage (puberty onwards)**: Mature sexual intimacy and adult personality formation.

Freud maintained that difficulties or conflicts in one stage could lead to "fixations" that shape adult personality traits or neuroses. The emphasis on early childhood experiences and the role of sexual energy (libido) was groundbreaking, though it provoked resistance in a culture that found discussions of childhood sexuality taboo.

15.3.3. Dream Analysis and the Unconscious

Freud's major work, **The Interpretation of Dreams** (1900), positioned **dreams** as the "royal road to the unconscious." He argued that repressed wishes, often of a sexual or aggressive nature, found symbolic expression in dreams. Dreams disguise these taboo impulses through symbolic transformations, allowing partial fulfillment without alerting the conscious mind.

Freud distinguished between a dream's **manifest content** (what is remembered upon waking) and its **latent content** (the hidden, unconscious meaning). Analyzing dreams—along with free associations and slips of the tongue ("Freudian slips")—became a cornerstone of psychoanalytic technique. By deciphering dream symbols, Freud believed one could unravel deeper personal conflicts and traumas.

15.3.4. Defense Mechanisms

Freud observed that the ego employs **defense mechanisms** to shield a person from anxiety arising out of internal conflicts or unacceptable impulses. Common defenses include:

- **Repression**: Pushing distressing thoughts into the unconscious.
- **Denial**: Refusing to acknowledge some aspect of reality.
- **Projection**: Attributing one's unacceptable impulses to others.
- **Displacement**: Redirecting impulses to a safer substitute target.
- **Reaction Formation**: Behaving opposite to one's true feelings to keep them hidden.

- **Rationalization**: Justifying behaviors or feelings with logical reasons, sidestepping the real unconscious motives.

Freud contended that while defenses might alleviate immediate anxiety, they could also produce psychological symptoms or relationship troubles in the long run. In therapy, making these defenses and underlying conflicts conscious was essential for healing.

15.4. Clinical Practice and the Psychoanalytic Setting

15.4.1. The Analytic Couch and Free Association

Freud's therapeutic approach typically placed the patient on a couch, with the analyst (Freud) seated out of direct view. This arrangement was designed to reduce inhibitions and encourage unfiltered speech. Patients were instructed to use **free association**—voicing any thought that came to mind, no matter how trivial or embarrassing.

The analyst listened for recurring themes, contradictions, or emotional reactions, formulating interpretations that pointed to hidden unconscious conflicts. The ultimate goal was to achieve **insight**: understanding how past traumas or internal conflicts shaped current symptoms. Through insight, patients might release repressed memories and restructure their emotional life.

15.4.2. Transference

In psychoanalysis, **transference** occurs when patients project feelings about significant people in their past (parents, siblings, or other figures) onto the analyst. For instance, a patient might interact with the analyst as if the latter were a critical father or a nurturing mother. Freud regarded transference as a crucial phenomenon: by analyzing these projections, one could uncover how the patient's early relationships shaped their ongoing relational patterns and conflicts.

Analysts were trained to recognize transference (and countertransference, their own emotional responses to the patient) to maintain the therapeutic process. The repeated re-enactment of core emotional dynamics within the therapy relationship could then be examined and gradually resolved, presumably allowing the patient more freedom from past attachments or resentments.

15.4.3. The Controversy Over Sexual Content

Freud's insistence on childhood sexuality and repressed sexual wishes as key factors in neuroses caused widespread scandal in conservative Vienna. Many of Freud's early lectures and publications were met with hostility or derision. Nevertheless, some physicians and intellectuals found his theories compelling, joining his circle to discuss psychoanalytic ideas. This group developed into the **Vienna Psychoanalytic Society**, forming the nucleus of the psychoanalytic movement.

However, disagreements soon arose over the central role of sexuality. Freud was adamant that libido, or sexual energy, was the fundamental driver of human behavior and psychological development. Others, including Carl Jung and Alfred Adler, doubted that sexuality was so universally dominant. These theoretical disputes led to major splits in the psychoanalytic community.

15.5. Carl Gustav Jung and Analytical Psychology

15.5.1. Jung's Early Collaboration with Freud

Carl Jung was a Swiss psychiatrist who showed an early interest in the unconscious, developing word-association tests to detect hidden emotional complexes. Impressed by Freud's work, Jung corresponded with him, and by 1907, the two formed a close professional bond. Freud hailed Jung as his "crown prince," hoping Jung's status at the Burghölzli psychiatric clinic in Zurich might help psychoanalysis gain broader medical acceptance.

However, despite a cordial beginning, Jung's theoretical differences with Freud emerged. He increasingly resisted Freud's emphasis on childhood sexuality, seeing it as too narrow. By 1913, the relationship deteriorated, resulting in a permanent schism.

15.5.2. Divergences from Freud

1. **Libido's Nature**: Jung viewed libido as a general life energy, not exclusively sexual. It encompassed creativity, spiritual impulses, and personal growth.
2. **Collective Unconscious**: While Freud's unconscious was primarily personal, filled with repressed individual conflicts, Jung proposed a **collective unconscious** shared by all humanity. This realm contained **archetypes**, universal symbolic themes such as the mother, hero, shadow, or anima/animus, manifesting in myths, dreams, and cultural motifs.
3. **Goal of Individuation**: Jung believed psychological growth involved integrating these unconscious archetypes into a coherent sense of self. He called this process **individuation**—becoming whole by reconciling conscious and unconscious elements.

Hence, Jung's **Analytical Psychology** moved away from Freud's focus on repressed sexuality and personal trauma, emphasizing spiritual and mythic dimensions of the psyche. He also used dream analysis, but with a broader interpretive lens that looked for archetypal imagery or universal patterns rather than purely personal repressed material.

15.5.3. Impact and Legacy

Jung's ideas gained traction among clinicians and philosophers intrigued by spirituality, myth, and creativity. Concepts like archetypes and the collective unconscious resonated with those seeking a more expansive understanding of the psyche. Jung's approach appealed to a range of fields: anthropology (myth study), religious studies, and artistic criticism.

However, critics found Jung's notions too speculative and lacking empirical support. Classical Freudians considered Jung's theories a dilution of the psychoanalytic core. Still, Jung's Analytical Psychology introduced a unique angle on the unconscious, broadening the scope of depth psychology beyond purely sexual or familial conflicts. Over time, Jung's influence spread globally, shaping many later schools of transpersonal or humanistic psychology.

15.6. Alfred Adler and Individual Psychology

15.6.1. Early Ties to Freud

Alfred Adler, an Austrian physician, joined Freud's discussion group in Vienna around 1902. Initially, Adler aligned with Freud's emphasis on unconscious motives in neurosis. Freud even named Adler president of the Vienna Psychoanalytic Society. However, Adler soon developed divergent views on the nature of human motivation, conflict, and social factors, leading to a split in 1911.

15.6.2. Core Ideas of Individual Psychology

Adler's "Individual Psychology" revolved around several main tenets:

1. **Striving for Superiority**: Whereas Freud saw sexual drives as central, Adler proposed that humans are primarily driven by a **will to power** or a desire to overcome feelings of inferiority. Children often feel small or helpless, motivating them to achieve competence, mastery, or social recognition.
2. **Social Interest**: Adler stressed the importance of **social interest**—a communal drive to cooperate and contribute to society. He believed psychological health hinged on balancing personal ambitions with social well-being.
3. **Birth Order and Family Dynamics**: Adler was one of the first to highlight how birth order might shape personality traits (e.g., firstborns might be more responsible or authority-seeking, middle children more competitive, youngest children more pampered or rebellious). While modern research presents mixed findings, Adler's emphasis on family context influenced subsequent developmental theories.
4. **Lifestyle**: Adler introduced the concept of "lifestyle" to describe an individual's unique way of pursuing goals and handling life's tasks. A "mistaken lifestyle" involved self-centered or socially harmful strategies, leading to neurosis.

In therapy, Adler focused on helping clients identify and correct faulty beliefs about themselves and society, fostering a more cooperative and confident approach to life's challenges.

15.6.3. Departure from Freud's Pessimistic View

Adler believed Freud's stress on internal conflict and sexual drives overlooked humans' capacity for social connection, creativity, and conscious decision-making. Adler's approach was more optimistic, underscoring personal growth and community feeling. This perspective appealed to many who found Freudian theory overly deterministic or cynical about human nature.

Like Jung, Adler broke from Freudian orthodoxy, establishing his own circle of followers. "Individual Psychology" influenced fields such as child guidance, education, and counseling. Many later psychologists—particularly in the United States—drew on Adler's focus on self-esteem, social belonging, and personal responsibility.

15.7. The Spread of Psychoanalysis

15.7.1. International Expansion

Despite internal rifts, psychoanalysis expanded in Europe and abroad. Freud's circle included figures like Sandor Ferenczi (Hungary), Karl Abraham (Germany), and Ernest Jones (Britain), all of whom carried psychoanalytic practice to their respective countries. Jones established the **British Psychoanalytical Society** and wrote a definitive biography of Freud.

After World War I, psychoanalytic societies formed in many European capitals, as well as in North and South America. Freud's writings were translated into multiple languages, spurring public debates about the unconscious, dream interpretation, and the role of sexuality in mental life.

15.7.2. Impact in the United States

The United States initially resisted psychoanalysis, with many American psychologists favoring laboratory-based experimental methods or the emerging Behaviorist movement. Nonetheless, psychiatrists—especially those on the East Coast—found Freud's approach compelling for treating neuroses and, later, for understanding war trauma (Shell Shock) after World War I. By the 1920s, New York and other major cities boasted analytic societies and training institutes.

Additionally, influential American intellectuals in literature, anthropology, and sociology cited Freudian ideas, weaving them into cultural critiques. Psychoanalytic theory influenced artistic movements, film, literary criticism, and popular media, spawning references to the "Oedipus complex" or repressed desires in everyday discourse.

15.8. Critiques and Controversies

15.8.1. Scientific Validity

From its inception, psychoanalysis faced scrutiny over the **scientific rigor** of its claims. Mainstream experimental psychologists argued that Freud's methods were anecdotal, reliant on subjective interpretations of clinical cases rather than controlled experiments. The reliance on "free association," dream analysis, and transference—none of which lent themselves to easy measurement—made psychoanalysis suspect in the eyes of those who demanded replicable, quantitative data.

Freud defended psychoanalysis as a "depth psychology," claiming it uncovered truths inaccessible to standard experimentation. However, critics noted the potential for **suggestion** or **observer bias** in the therapist's interpretations. Additionally, Freud's theories were seen as **unfalsifiable**—capable of explaining any outcome in retrospect, thus resisting objective testing.

15.8.2. Cultural Resistance and Accusations of Pessimism

Freud's emphasis on infantile sexuality, aggression, and repressed conflicts alarmed many in Europe's conservative circles. Religious authorities and moral traditionalists attacked psychoanalysis as subversive or immoral. Others found the portrayal of humans as largely driven by unconscious lusts and fears excessively pessimistic.

Freud's defenders argued that acknowledging hidden drives could free individuals from destructive neuroses. Still, social tensions remained high, and some psychoanalysts faced professional ostracism. Jung's and Adler's more expansive visions—incorporating spirituality, social interest, or general "life energy"—offered alternatives that some found less disturbing or fatalistic.

15.9. Long-Term Influence of Psychoanalysis

Despite controversies, psychoanalysis left an indelible mark on psychology and Western culture more broadly:

1. **Expansion of Mental Health Treatment**: Freud's model legitimized lengthy, talk-based therapies. Previously, hysterical or neurotic patients might have been dismissed or institutionalized without comprehensive psychological intervention. Psychoanalysis suggested that in-depth dialogue could uncover and heal core conflicts.
2. **Focus on Childhood and Development**: Psychoanalysis underscored the significance of early childhood experiences and the family dynamic in shaping adult personality. Even rival theories (e.g., Behaviorism, Developmental Psychology) took up the theme of childhood as crucial to later outcomes.
3. **Unconscious Processes in the Arts and Humanities**: Writers, artists, and filmmakers drew heavily on Freudian ideas about dream symbolism, hidden motives, and sexual tensions. This cross-pollination shaped entire artistic movements, from Surrealism to modernist literature.

4. **Influence on Subsequent Therapies**: Many 20th-century therapeutic schools—Object Relations, Ego Psychology, Self Psychology—extended or revised Freud's basic tenets, maintaining some form of psychoanalytic framework while refining or disagreeing with specific points. Even newer approaches (Humanistic, Cognitive) often define themselves in response to psychoanalytic concepts.

In sum, Freud's notion of the unconscious irrevocably expanded psychological inquiry beyond conscious introspection or overt behavior. Jung's and Adler's revisions, though separate, further diversified psychoanalytic thought, incorporating spirituality, life goals, and social context. By the early 20th century, psychoanalysis stood as a major clinical and cultural force—coexisting, sometimes uneasily, with academic experimental psychology.

CHAPTER 16: EARLY BEHAVIORISM

16.1. Introduction

Around the turn of the 20th century, dissatisfaction with introspection and psychoanalytic speculation led some psychologists to propose a radical alternative: focus on **observable behavior** rather than subjective experience. This shift crystallized into the **Behaviorist** movement, which sought to make psychology as objective and scientific as possible by measuring stimuli and responses—leaving behind consciousness, the unconscious, and internal mental states as unverifiable constructs.

Although **John B. Watson** typically gets credit for launching Behaviorism in 1913, the movement had roots in the work of **Edward Thorndike** (studying animal intelligence) and **Ivan Pavlov** (researching conditioned reflexes). By spotlighting learning processes observable in experiments, these pioneers believed they had found a foundation for psychology that rivaled older approaches (Structuralism, Functionalism, Psychoanalysis). This chapter examines how early Behaviorism arose, shaped research on animal and human learning, and challenged the entire field to reevaluate its methods and subject matter.

16.2. Edward Thorndike

16.2.1. Early Life and the Puzzle Box Experiments

Edward Lee Thorndike (1874–1949) was an American psychologist who bridged the gap between Functionalism and the emerging

Behaviorist ethos. As a graduate student at Harvard under William James, Thorndike became interested in how animals solve problems. He transferred to Columbia University, conducting his famous "puzzle box" research for his dissertation.

Thorndike's **puzzle boxes** were simple contraptions where a cat, for instance, was placed inside and needed to manipulate a latch or lever to escape and obtain food. Initially, the cat's behavior was random—scratching, meowing, sniffing—until it accidentally triggered the correct response. Over successive trials, the cat's time to escape decreased, suggesting it had "learned" which behavior led to a reward.

16.2.2. The Law of Effect

From his puzzle box experiments, Thorndike formulated the **Law of Effect** (1898). It states that if a response in the presence of a stimulus leads to a satisfying or "annoying" outcome, the connection (or "bond") between the stimulus and that response becomes either strengthened or weakened. Essentially:

- **Behaviors followed by pleasant consequences** become more likely to occur again.
- **Behaviors followed by unpleasant consequences** become less likely.

This principle foreshadowed the central behaviorist idea that learning depends on reinforcement or punishment. Thorndike's notion of **connectionism** emphasized direct bonds formed between stimuli and successful responses—bypassing any need to invoke conscious ideas or emotions. Thus, Thorndike's work shifted psychology toward a more mechanical, trial-and-error explanation of learning.

16.2.3. Educational Applications

Thorndike was also a key figure in applying psychological findings to education. He believed that human learning resembled animal learning in that practice and reward shaped habit formation. In his book **Educational Psychology** (1903), Thorndike argued for teaching methods that provide clear objectives, repeated practice, and immediate feedback on performance. He designed standardized tests to measure students' abilities, championing a data-driven approach to school curricula.

Though some found his methods overly mechanistic, Thorndike's emphasis on measurable outcomes heavily influenced 20th-century education. He helped found the field of **educational psychology** as a distinct discipline, extending behavioral principles into classrooms.

16.3. Ivan Pavlov

16.3.1. Physiological Research and the Discovery of Conditioned Reflexes

Ivan Petrovich Pavlov (1849–1936) was a Russian physiologist, not originally a psychologist. He spent years investigating digestion in dogs, measuring saliva production in response to food. During these experiments, Pavlov noticed that his laboratory dogs began salivating **before** tasting the food—sometimes upon merely seeing the lab assistant who fed them. Intrigued, he turned his attention to the phenomenon of "psychic secretions."

Pavlov systematically presented a **neutral stimulus** (e.g., a buzzer or bell) immediately before giving food. After several pairings, the dogs would salivate upon hearing the bell alone, indicating they had formed a new reflex. Pavlov called this process **classical conditioning** (or **Pavlovian conditioning**). He distinguished:

- **Unconditioned Stimulus (US)**: Food, which naturally elicits salivation (the Unconditioned Response, UR).
- **Neutral Stimulus (NS)**: A bell or tone, which initially does not cause salivation.
- **Conditioned Stimulus (CS)**: The bell, after repeated pairing with the food.
- **Conditioned Response (CR)**: Salivation triggered by the bell alone.

16.3.2. Processes of Conditioning

Pavlov explored multiple dimensions of this learning process:

- **Acquisition**: The stage in which repeated NS–US pairings form the CR.
- **Extinction**: If the CS is presented repeatedly without the US, the CR weakens and eventually stops.
- **Spontaneous Recovery**: Even after extinction, a rest period may see the CR reappear when the CS is presented again, though usually weaker.
- **Generalization**: A dog conditioned to salivate at a specific tone might also salivate to similar tones.
- **Discrimination**: If only one tone is paired with food while another is never followed by food, the dog learns to respond to the first tone but not the second.

While Pavlov's research was purely physiological, its implications for psychology were profound. It demonstrated how **associative learning** could be systematically studied in the lab, providing an objective framework for analyzing behavior without recourse to introspection or unconscious processes.

16.3.3. Influence on Psychology

Pavlov's conditioning model fascinated many early 20th-century psychologists, especially in the U.S. His experiments showed that behavior could be predicted and controlled by manipulating environmental stimuli and reinforcement. This data-driven, objective approach resonated with the emerging Behaviorist mindset.

Although Pavlov never fully identified with psychological theories per se—preferring the label "physiologist"—his "conditioned reflex" concept became a cornerstone of behaviorist research, eventually applied to understanding phobias, habit formation, and even advertising strategies (by pairing products with pleasant stimuli). Pavlov's careful methods and quantitative measures exemplified how one could dissect learning processes without referencing intangible mental states.

16.4. John B. Watson

16.4.1. Background and Key Influences

John Broadus Watson (1878–1958) was an American psychologist who initially studied with **John Dewey** (a Functionalist) and later influenced by Pavlov's findings. Watson believed that psychology needed to abandon all references to consciousness, introspection, and mental images if it wished to be truly scientific.

Like Thorndike, Watson performed animal studies—researching how rats navigated mazes. He found that rats required sense cues (proprioception, smell, vision) to learn the maze, but once they learned, they seemed to rely mainly on simpler motor habits. This reinforced Watson's conviction that complicated "mental processes" could be explained through associations between stimuli and responses.

16.4.2. The 1913 Behaviorist Manifesto

Watson formally launched **Behaviorism** with his paper "Psychology as the Behaviorist Views It," published in **Psychological Review** in 1913. Often called the "Behaviorist Manifesto," this article declared:

1. Psychology should be a **purely objective** branch of science, studying behavior, not mental states.
2. The goal of psychology is to **predict and control** behavior, rather than describe consciousness.
3. Introspection is untrustworthy; data must come from **observable** and **measurable** phenomena.
4. Human and animal behavior should be studied under similar principles, as they both form habits through environmental conditioning.

This was a direct challenge to Structuralism, Functionalism, and Psychoanalysis, all of which used introspection or subjective interpretation. Watson insisted that psychology, to be on par with physics or chemistry, must ignore the intangible "mind" and focus exclusively on external, quantifiable processes.

16.4.3. The "Little Albert" Experiment

One of Watson's most famous (and ethically controversial) experiments was the **"Little Albert" study (1920)**, conducted with his graduate student Rosalie Rayner. They sought to show how fear could be **classically conditioned** in a young child. Little Albert, approximately 11 months old, was presented with a white rat (initially a neutral stimulus). While he reached for the rat, Watson struck a steel bar behind the child's head, producing a loud, frightening noise (the unconditioned stimulus). After several pairings, Albert began to cry and show fear responses whenever he saw the rat alone, now a conditioned stimulus.

Furthermore, Albert's fear generalized to other white, furry objects. Although the experiment was never systematically "unconditioned," it implied that phobias might arise through learned associations rather than innate predispositions or repressed conflicts. This finding was a stark contrast to psychoanalytic interpretations of fear. However, modern ethics standards severely criticize the study for causing distress without proper informed consent or deconditioning.

16.4.4. Popularizing Behaviorism

Watson wrote for academic and popular audiences, championing the idea that if psychologists controlled the environment, they could shape infants into "any type of specialist" through training—an extreme environmental determinism. He left academia in 1920 after a scandalous divorce but continued to promote Behaviorist ideas in advertising, applying stimulus-response conditioning to consumer behavior.

Watson's rhetorical skill and flair for publicity helped Behaviorism gain public attention, overshadowing introspective psychology in many U.S. universities by the 1920s and 1930s. The promise that careful manipulation of stimuli and reinforcers could mold any behavior appealed to progressive educators, industrial managers, and social planners who sought efficient, "scientific" methods for shaping habits.

16.5. Key Principles of Early Behaviorism

16.5.1. Stimulus-Response (S-R) Psychology

At its core, early Behaviorism championed the Stimulus-Response model:

- **Stimulus (S)**: An external event or cue in the environment.
- **Response (R)**: An observable action or behavior triggered by the stimulus.

Behaviorists saw all learning as the strengthening or weakening of S-R bonds through reinforcement or punishment. The approach minimized or outright dismissed the role of mental states. If an organism changed behavior after repeated experiences, the explanation lay in altered S-R connections, not in introspective revelations or unconscious conflicts.

In practical research, behaviorists tested animals (rats, dogs, pigeons) in controlled apparatus to measure how changes in reinforcement schedules (e.g., consistent reward, partial reward) affected performance. They believed these laws would generalize to humans, explaining everything from language acquisition to emotional attachments.

16.5.2. Rejection of Instinct and Innate Ideas

Early Behaviorists contended that most (if not all) behavior was learned through conditioning, challenging views that large portions of human behavior were guided by instincts or inborn tendencies. For instance, Watson argued that so-called "instinctive" emotional responses were modifiable through experience.

This blank-slate perspective dovetailed with John Locke's empiricism from two centuries earlier, yet it was expressed in rigorous, laboratory-based language. Behaviorists insisted that with the right conditions, any creature could learn virtually any response to any stimulus. While subsequent research would show biological constraints on learning, early Behaviorism championed a near-limitless malleability of behavior under environmental influence.

16.5.3. Focus on Animal Research

Behaviorists, following Thorndike and Pavlov, viewed animal experiments as the gold standard because they allowed strict control over variables. Studying how rats run through mazes or how dogs salivate to bells eliminated complexities of human introspection, making for "clean" data.

Watson extended this logic to humans, seeing no fundamental difference in learning mechanisms across species. He insisted that by unveiling universal S-R laws in animals, psychologists could apply them to child-rearing, education, therapy, or advertising. This approach shaped a generation of graduate research: rat mazes, puzzle boxes, lever-pressing apparatus, all to decode the laws of habit formation.

16.6. Early Applications and Extensions

16.6.1. Child-Rearing Advice

Watson famously applied Behaviorist principles to parenting. In his book **Psychological Care of Infant and Child** (1928), he discouraged displays of affection or coddling children, suggesting it might produce dependency or emotional instability. Instead, he advocated a systematic approach with consistent rewards for desired behaviors and mild, measured punishments for undesired ones—akin to training animals.

Though this advice was widely read, many criticized it as cold or mechanical, ignoring children's emotional needs beyond S-R contingencies. Yet it exemplified the ambition of Behaviorism to reorganize society using scientific methods.

16.6.2. Advertising and Consumer Behavior

When Watson joined the advertising firm J. Walter Thompson, he applied conditioning to shape consumer preferences. Products were paired with images or slogans evoking positive emotional responses (similar to Pavlov's classical conditioning). This approach became standard marketing practice: commercials might show happy families or attractive models to associate good feelings with a brand, hoping to trigger purchase reflexes.

Thus, Behaviorist ideas spread beyond academia into the commercial world, reinforcing the notion that behavior could be engineered by controlling stimuli and reinforcement. Watson's success in advertising demonstrated Behaviorism's pragmatic potential and the cultural appetite for such "scientific" manipulation of human habits.

16.7. Critiques of Early Behaviorism

16.7.1. Neglect of Internal States

Psychoanalysts, cognitive-oriented psychologists (still nascent at the time), and even some Functionalists criticized Behaviorists for **ignoring the "black box"** of mental life. They argued that emotions, motives, and complex thought processes played a vital role in behavior—yet Behaviorists dismissed these as epiphenomena unworthy of scientific study.

Skeptics contended that certain phenomena—language, problem-solving, imagination—cannot be easily reduced to simple S-R laws. They also noted that some learning occurs without immediate reinforcement, pointing to latent or observational learning. Critics thus found the Behaviorist framework too restrictive to account for all aspects of human psychology.

16.7.2. Overly Simplistic Extrapolations

Some scholars felt that equating human behavior to rat or dog behavior overlooked the complexities of culture, reasoning, and self-awareness. Behaviorists responded that the basic laws of learning are universal, though the contexts differ. But critics insisted that phenomena like grammar acquisition or symbolic thinking might require innate structures or mental representations, refuting a pure tabula rasa stance.

Nevertheless, early Behaviorism's success in controlling and predicting certain behaviors in labs and real-world settings gave it considerable influence. By the 1930s, Behaviorism dominated many American psychology departments, overshadowing introspective or psychoanalytic approaches. Scholars like B.F. Skinner (though slightly later) would refine Behaviorist methods, focusing on operant conditioning—a development we will see in Chapter 17.

16.8. Broader Impact and Transition

By the late 1920s and early 1930s, the Behaviorist movement had several established tenets:

1. **Learning is the key** to all (or nearly all) behavioral change.
2. **Environment shapes behavior** through reinforcement or punishment.
3. **Research should rely on objective measures** (reaction times, error rates, frequency of responses) rather than subjective reports.
4. **Humans differ from animals in complexity, not in fundamental learning principles**.

This approach heavily influenced educational practices, therapy techniques (particularly later forms of behavior therapy), and experimental designs in psychology. Yet even as Behaviorism rose, critiques emerged, including from the **Gestalt** tradition in Germany (Chapter 18) and from psychologists who studied complex cognition or emotion. Eventually, these critiques would intensify, leading to modifications and expansions of Behaviorism into other frameworks that recognized internal processes, culminating in the "Cognitive Revolution" of the mid-20th century.

Within the historical arc covered in this book, we see how Behaviorism addressed the dissatisfaction with earlier reliance on introspection, forging a robust, data-driven approach. It aligned with the scientific climate of the early 20th century, emphasizing precision, measurement, and the possibility of controlling behavior through systematic manipulation of environmental factors. This radical stance shaped American psychology for decades, revolutionizing both academic research and practical applications—yet also leaving out aspects of mental life that cannot be directly observed.

CHAPTER 17: BEHAVIORISM UNDER B.F. SKINNER

17.1. Introduction

By the 1930s, **Behaviorism** was well-established in American psychology, thanks in large part to John B. Watson's forceful advocacy and the foundational work of Edward Thorndike and Ivan Pavlov. Yet the next major phase of behaviorist thought would be led by **Burrhus Frederic Skinner (1904–1990)**, who developed an innovative framework called **operant conditioning**. Skinner shifted the focus from classical (Pavlovian) conditioning—where reflexes are elicited by preceding stimuli—to how behavior is influenced by **consequences** that follow.

Through decades of systematic research, Skinner introduced ideas like **reinforcement**, **punishment**, **shaping**, and **schedules of reinforcement**. He constructed laboratory apparatus, notably the "Skinner box," to study how animals learn or sustain various behaviors under controlled contingencies. Over time, Skinner extended these principles to explain human behavior in everyday life, championing a radical stance that all behavior—human or animal—could be understood through environmental histories of reinforcement and punishment.

This chapter traces Skinner's background, the essence of operant conditioning, and the broader impact of his radical behaviorism. We will see how his approach dominated mid-20th-century American psychology, branching into educational practices, therapy methods, and even social engineering proposals. While critics argued that Skinner's views minimized the role of internal processes or free will, his data-driven research and practical applications influenced generations of psychologists, shaping the discipline in profound ways.

17.2. Early Life and Intellectual Influences

17.2.1. Skinner's Academic Path

B.F. Skinner was born in Susquehanna, Pennsylvania, in 1904. As a child, he tinkered with mechanical gadgets and displayed curiosity about how things worked. He enrolled at Hamilton College intending to become a writer, but after reading about Pavlov's conditioning experiments and John B. Watson's vision, he felt drawn to psychology's scientific possibilities.

Skinner joined the psychology graduate program at Harvard University, where he studied with figures influenced by behaviorism. He completed his Ph.D. in 1931, focusing on the relationship between reflexes and environmental stimuli, although he was already moving beyond classical conditioning toward a concept he would soon call **operant conditioning**. During a postdoctoral fellowship at Harvard, Skinner refined his experimental methods, developing apparatus that allowed precise measurement of an animal's ongoing behavior and the immediate consequences that shaped it.

17.2.2. From Reflexes to Operants

In classical (Pavlovian) conditioning, an organism learns associations between two stimuli—one initially neutral (like a tone) and one inherently meaningful (like food)—so that the neutral stimulus eventually elicits a reflex response (salivation). Skinner realized that much of everyday behavior did not fit the reflex model. People and animals often act spontaneously, and their actions produce consequences. This is not a matter of eliciting a reflex but rather the

emission of a behavior that is subsequently selected or discarded based on its outcomes.

Skinner borrowed the term "operant" to emphasize that the behavior "operates" on the environment to produce consequences. Over the next decades, Skinner would systematically investigate these operant behaviors, eventually building a broad theoretical framework for how environmental contingencies shape learning.

17.3. The Operant Conditioning Paradigm

17.3.1. The Skinner Box

To study operant behavior rigorously, Skinner designed a laboratory apparatus known colloquially as the **"Skinner box."** Typically, it's a chamber equipped with:

- **A lever or key**: The animal (rat, pigeon) can manipulate it.
- **A mechanism to deliver reinforcers** (food pellets, water).
- **A recording device** to track each lever press or key peck.

By precisely controlling when reinforcement (food) was delivered and tracking how often the animal responded, Skinner could identify how environmental contingencies influenced the frequency of that operant (lever-pressing or key-pecking). This direct measurement of behavior—without inferring internal states—embodied the behaviorist emphasis on observable data.

17.3.2. Reinforcement: Positive and Negative

A central concept in operant conditioning is **reinforcement**: any consequence that strengthens or increases the likelihood of the behavior it follows. Skinner distinguished:

1. **Positive Reinforcement**: Presenting a pleasant stimulus after a behavior (e.g., giving food to a rat). The behavior is more likely to recur because it yields a reward.
2. **Negative Reinforcement**: Removing an unpleasant stimulus after a behavior (e.g., stopping a mild electric shock when the rat presses the lever). This also increases the likelihood of the behavior because it terminates something aversive.

Both positive and negative reinforcement result in heightened frequency of the operant. In daily human life, positive reinforcers might be compliments or paychecks, while negative reinforcers could be relief from chores, pain, or annoyances once a certain action is performed.

17.3.3. Punishment

In contrast to reinforcement, **punishment** is a consequence that decreases the likelihood of a behavior. Skinner noted two main forms:

- **Positive Punishment**: Administering an aversive stimulus following a response (e.g., scolding a child, delivering a mild shock).
- **Negative Punishment** (also called response cost): Removing a pleasant stimulus following a response (e.g., taking away a favorite toy, revoking privileges).

Though punishment can suppress behavior, Skinner was wary of its side effects—fear, aggression, avoidance—arguing that reinforcement was generally more effective and ethically preferable for shaping behavior.

17.3.4. Shaping and Successive Approximations

One of Skinner's significant insights was **shaping**: reinforcing small steps or "successive approximations" toward a target behavior. Instead of waiting for an animal to randomly perform a complex action, the experimenter rewards simpler actions that resemble the final behavior, gradually raising the criterion.

For example, to train a pigeon to spin in a circle, one might first reinforce the pigeon for turning its head slightly to the left. Once that's established, only turning a bit further is rewarded, and so on, until the pigeon completes a full rotation. Skinner showed that by carefully controlling reinforcers, even intricate behaviors could be built up systematically—no appeal to conscious thought or hidden motives was necessary.

17.4. Schedules of Reinforcement

17.4.1. Continuous vs. Partial Reinforcement

Skinner's research also revealed that how reinforcers are scheduled has profound effects on behavior:

- **Continuous Reinforcement (CRF)**: Every correct response earns a reinforcer. This typically accelerates learning but is vulnerable to rapid extinction if reinforcers stop.
- **Partial (Intermittent) Reinforcement**: Reinforcers are given only some of the time, based on different rules. Although acquisition might be slower, partial reinforcement leads to greater **resistance to extinction** because organisms become accustomed to responding without immediate reward.

Within partial reinforcement, Skinner identified specific schedules:

1. **Fixed Ratio (FR)**: Reinforcement occurs after a set number of responses (e.g., FR-10 means a reward after every 10 lever presses).
2. **Variable Ratio (VR)**: Reinforcement occurs after a varying number of responses, centered around an average (e.g., VR-10

means on average every 10 presses, but sometimes after 5, sometimes after 15, etc.).
3. **Fixed Interval (FI)**: Reinforcement becomes available after a fixed amount of time (e.g., FI-30 seconds: first correct response after 30 seconds is rewarded).
4. **Variable Interval (VI)**: Reinforcement is available after a variable time interval around some mean (VI-30 means on average 30 seconds, but sometimes 10, sometimes 50).

17.4.2. Behavioral Patterns Under Each Schedule

Skinner discovered characteristic patterns of responding under different schedules:

- **Ratio Schedules** generally produce high response rates, because reinforcers depend on work output. Under VR schedules (like gambling slot machines), behavior can be especially persistent and resistant to extinction due to the unpredictability of payoff.
- **Interval Schedules** often produce "scalloped" patterns (especially FI), where responses slow after a reward and then accelerate as the next interval nears completion.

By charting these response curves on a cumulative recorder, Skinner showed that behavior was systematically governed by the rules of reinforcement, highlighting how environmental contingencies shape rates and patterns of responding—even in the absence of conscious planning.

17.5. Radical Behaviorism and Beyond

17.5.1. The Philosophy of Radical Behaviorism

Skinner's stance, often called **"radical behaviorism,"** proposed that internal events such as thoughts, emotions, or intentions are themselves forms of behavior—subject to the same laws of learning as overt actions. He argued that while these private events occur within the skin, they do not require a separate realm of "mind." Instead, they are simply covert responses shaped by genetics and the environment.

In Skinner's view, consciousness or free will did not stand as distinct causal forces. He believed that every act, whether private or public, was ultimately determined by one's history of reinforcement in combination with genetic endowment. This perspective contradicted centuries of philosophical assumptions about free agency, sparking debates on morality, personal responsibility, and creativity.

17.5.2. Language and Verbal Behavior

Skinner ventured into the domain of human language in his book **Verbal Behavior** (1957), applying operant principles to speech and communication. He categorized speech acts as **mands** (requests), **tacts** (labels), **intraverbals** (responses to other verbal stimuli), and so forth, all shaped by social reinforcement.

For instance, a child says "cookie" in the presence of a cookie and receives praise or the cookie itself—reinforcing the verbal behavior. Over time, more complex utterances develop by chaining smaller verbal units, each reinforced in context. By ignoring mentalistic explanations of language, Skinner caused controversies: critics (most famously linguist Noam Chomsky in a later era) argued that language involved innate structures and generative grammar, far beyond simple reinforcement. However, within the mid-20th-century context, Skinner's attempt to systematically explain verbal behavior in purely behavioral terms was pathbreaking.

17.5.3. Applications to Society

Skinner believed that harnessing operant conditioning could improve human welfare. In **Walden Two** (1948), a utopian novel, he depicted a community governed by positive reinforcement—eliminating punitive methods, fostering cooperation, and carefully designing educational and social practices.

He also promoted **behavior modification** or **behavior therapy**, which used reinforcement and punishment contingencies to address behavioral problems in clinical settings. For example, children with developmental issues or individuals with phobias could benefit from carefully arranged reinforcement for desired actions. Skinnerian methods also influenced business management (employee incentive programs), education (personalized instruction, token economies), and beyond.

17.6. Reactions and Criticisms

17.6.1. Cognitivist Objections

Even during Skinner's heyday, some psychologists began emphasizing **cognitive** processes—mental representations, problem-solving strategies, memory encoding—that could not be fully explained by a purely S-R or reinforcement-based model. Edward Tolman, for instance, studied **cognitive maps** in rats, showing that they could learn maze layouts without direct reinforcement.

Tolman's findings hinted that animals' internal representations guided behavior, challenging strict behaviorist claims that only external contingencies mattered. While Tolman considered himself a "purposive behaviorist," his ideas paved the way for a broader cognitive revolution (which would bloom more fully after the mid-20th century).

17.6.2. Ethical and Philosophical Debates

Some philosophers and laypeople viewed Skinner's claim that all behavior is determined by environment as an attack on human dignity or free will. They argued that morality, creativity, and personal agency seemed incompatible with the radical behaviorist stance, which reduces actions to learned patterns shaped by reinforcement.

Skinner responded that acknowledging environmental causation does not degrade human accomplishments; rather, it illuminates how achievements come about, enabling more effective social design. Nonetheless, critics worried that a society built on operant principles might slide into authoritarianism if "controllers" manipulated masses for their own ends—echoing dystopian fears.

17.6.3. Narrow Focus on Observable Behavior

Whereas psychoanalysis and other depth psychologies probed unconscious conflicts, Skinner largely dismissed them as untestable hypotheses. He insisted that mentalistic constructs add confusion, not clarity, to scientific inquiry. But critics pointed out that ignoring emotions, subjective experiences, and internal motivations might oversimplify the complexities of real human life.

Still, Skinner's careful experiments on how schedules of reinforcement shape persistent patterns of behavior carried immense weight, demonstrating that large swaths of learning could be explained with no recourse to introspection or unmeasured variables. Many found this approach compelling for generating reliable, replicable data.

17.7. Contributions to Psychological Science

Despite controversies, Skinner's influence was profound:

1. **Rigorous Experimental Method**: By measuring response rates under precise reinforcement schedules, Skinner established a model for how to do behavioral research systematically.
2. **Operant Principles**: Concepts of reinforcement, punishment, shaping, and extinction remain cornerstones of learning theory, widely used in animal training, behavior therapy, and educational programs.
3. **Beyond the Lab**: Skinner's vision extended into applied fields—behavior modification in mental health institutions, token economies for classroom management, systematic instruction in educational programs, and more.
4. **Challenging the Role of Internal States**: Whether one agrees with radical behaviorism or not, Skinner forced psychologists to refine how they conceptualize the relationship between external contingencies and inner experiences.

During the mid-20th century, Skinner's brand of Behaviorism—often called the "**experimental analysis of behavior**"—became a powerful paradigm in American psychology, overshadowing older introspective methods and even psychoanalysis in many university departments. It coexisted with other forms of behavioral research, such as Clark Hull's drive-reduction theory or Edward Tolman's cognitive behaviorism, but Skinner's radical stance, combined with his unwavering devotion to data, gave him a unique position in shaping the discourse.

17.8. Later Developments and Legacy

17.8.1. Behavior Analysis

As Skinner's ideas spread, a new field—**Behavior Analysis**—emerged, focusing on discovering lawful relationships between environmental events and behavior. Professional organizations, like the Association for Behavior Analysis, formed, and journals published experimental findings about operant processes in both animal and human contexts.

By designing elaborate reinforcement contingencies, researchers tackled issues of self-control (delaying immediate rewards for greater long-term benefits), problem-solving, and even language in nonhuman species. Some labs trained pigeons to discriminate complex visual patterns or to perform sequences of tasks—demonstrations that showcased how far shaping and reinforcement could go in generating sophisticated behaviors.

17.8.2. Clinical and Educational Interventions

Behavior therapy developed from Skinner's principles. Therapists working with phobias, anxiety, or habit disorders used systematic **desensitization**, **token economies**, **contingency contracts**, and **applied behavior analysis (ABA)** techniques. For instance, in the 1960s and 1970s, Ivar Lovaas applied operant methods to children with autism, focusing on building communication skills through consistent reinforcement.

In the classroom, **programmed instruction** was championed: materials were broken into small steps, each requiring an active response from the learner, followed by immediate feedback. This approach aimed to "shape" academic skills incrementally. While later educational theories integrated more cognitive elements, the emphasis on incremental skill-building and feedback owes much to Skinner's influence.

17.8.3. The Rise of Cognitive Alternatives

By the 1960s, the so-called **"cognitive revolution"** gained momentum, introducing mental constructs—such as memory stores, schemas, or information processing models—back into psychology. Behaviorism never entirely vanished, but many psychologists concluded that some phenomena (e.g., language, problem-solving, concept formation) required theoretical constructs beyond S-R contingencies.

Still, Skinner's methods survived in subfields focusing on practical outcomes: training animals for search-and-rescue, developing effective therapies for behavioral disorders, designing user-friendly systems guided by the principle of reinforcement for correct usage. Even though mainstream academic psychology shifted to cognitive frameworks, **behavior analysis** remained robust, supported by specialized journals, societies, and practitioners who found operant principles highly effective for certain goals.

CHAPTER 18: GESTALT PSYCHOLOGY

18.1. Introduction

While Behaviorism reigned in the United States by the 1920s and 1930s, another influential movement was taking shape in Germany: **Gestalt Psychology**. Led by **Max Wertheimer (1880–1943)**, **Kurt Koffka (1886–1941)**, and **Wolfgang Köhler (1887–1967)**, Gestalt psychologists argued that we perceive and think about the world in **organized wholes**, not merely as sums of discrete parts. The term "*gestalt*" in German roughly translates to "form," "shape," or "configuration."

Reacting against earlier atomistic approaches—such as structuralism, which dissected the mind into elemental sensations—Gestalt psychologists insisted on studying how the mind actively organizes and interprets sensory information. They discovered fundamental principles of perception, demonstrating that we automatically group stimuli into coherent patterns, interpret ambiguous figures in certain ways, and resolve incomplete forms into wholes.

This chapter explores Gestalt psychology's founding experiments, core perceptual principles (e.g., figure-ground, proximity, similarity, closure), and how researchers extended these ideas to problem-solving and learning (Köhler's studies of insight in apes). Forced to emigrate during the Nazi era, many Gestalt psychologists carried their theories to the United States, influencing broader trends in perception research, social psychology, and later the cognitive revolution. Though overshadowed by Behaviorism in mid-century American psychology, Gestalt's legacy endured, shaping how scientists and the public understand perception and creativity.

18.2. The Founders and Early Milestones

18.2.1. Max Wertheimer: The Phi Phenomenon

Gestalt psychology began in 1912 with **Max Wertheimer's** publication on the **phi phenomenon**, which involves the illusion of motion when two stationary lights flash on and off in rapid succession. Observing a demonstration with flashing lights on a train journey, Wertheimer noticed that under certain temporal intervals, a viewer perceives continuous motion between the lights, rather than two separate flickers.

Wertheimer's experiments with carefully timed light flashes revealed that the perceived movement is not reducible to the sum of individual sensations (light #1, then light #2). Instead, the mind organizes these stimuli into a singular experience of motion—a *gestalt* that is distinct from any single static element. This finding challenged the notion that perception can be explained by associating discrete sensory bits. Instead, the conscious experience arises from the pattern or configuration.

18.2.2. Kurt Koffka and Wolfgang Köhler Join the Movement

Wertheimer soon collaborated with **Kurt Koffka** and **Wolfgang Köhler**. Together, they elaborated on the principles of Gestalt psychology in perception, learning, and problem-solving. In 1912, Koffka published a major review article on Gestalt principles, raising international awareness of the new movement. Köhler further advanced these ideas in his experimental work with animals, focusing on **insightful learning**.

All three were based in Germany—at Frankfurt, Berlin, and Giessen—where they refined Gestalt theories against the backdrop of other influential German traditions (such as Wundtian psychology and the rising interest in phenomenology). By the 1920s, Gestalt psychology became a recognized school, widely taught in German universities.

18.2.3. Emigration and Influence

In the early 1930s, the Nazi regime's policies forced many Jewish or politically dissident academics to flee Germany. Wertheimer, Koffka, and Köhler emigrated to the United States, bringing Gestalt theories to American academic circles. While overshadowed by Behaviorism's dominance, their work on perception and cognition attracted a niche following, influencing later developments in social psychology, personality theory, and eventually the cognitive revolution.

Though the Gestalt movement never formed a large institutional presence in America akin to Behaviorism or Psychoanalysis, it left a lasting intellectual mark, particularly in research on perception and problem-solving. Some of the greatest achievements of mid-20th-century American psychology (e.g., in social cognition, group dynamics, or visual illusions) drew upon Gestalt insights.

18.3. Core Principles of Gestalt Perception

At the heart of Gestalt psychology lies the idea that the **mind actively organizes** stimuli into meaningful wholes. This is not a passive assembly of sensory bits, but an innate process that imposes structure on the input. Several **Gestalt principles** describe how we group stimuli:

1. **Figure-Ground**: We naturally separate a visual scene into a **figure** (an object of focus) and the **ground** (the background). Sometimes figure and ground can reverse, as in "ambiguous figures," but typically one region stands out as the focal shape while the rest recedes.
2. **Proximity**: Elements close to each other tend to be perceived as part of the same group.
3. **Similarity**: We group items that share visual characteristics (e.g., color, shape) together.
4. **Closure**: We tend to "close" gaps in an incomplete figure, perceiving it as a coherent whole.
5. **Continuity** (or Good Continuation): We prefer continuous forms rather than abrupt changes in direction. Lines are seen as following the smoothest path.
6. **Symmetry**: Symmetrical regions are often seen as belonging together, forming coherent shapes.
7. **Common Fate**: Elements moving in the same direction or at the same speed are grouped as a single entity.

18.3.1. Holistic Perception

Each principle reflects the **holistic** nature of perception: the mind does not add up small parts to form a picture; instead, it spontaneously organizes stimuli into structured patterns. A classic demonstration is the **Necker cube**, an ambiguous line drawing of a cube that can flip back and forth in depth orientation. Gestalt psychologists emphasized that the brain jumps between interpretations, each forming a stable whole, rather than mixing them.

18.3.2. Prägnanz (Good Figure)

Gestaltists proposed the law of **Prägnanz**, meaning the mind seeks the simplest, most stable form. When confronted with ambiguous or incomplete visual data, perception favors the "best" or "most coherent" figure. This principle underlies illusions where the visual system reconstructs a simplified or symmetrical pattern out of partial cues.

Thus, experience is not just passively recorded; it's an **active** reconstruction where the mind aims for clarity and order. This concept of self-organization in perception was novel, contrasting with older approaches that claimed complex perceptions derived from learned associations between simpler sensations.

18.4. Insights into Problem-Solving

18.4.1. The Canary Islands Research

Wolfgang Köhler worked at the Prussian Academy of Sciences station in Tenerife (Canary Islands) during World War I. There, he studied chimpanzees in captivity, investigating how they solved tasks such as retrieving bananas placed out of immediate reach. He published these findings in **The Mentality of Apes (1917)**, which became a cornerstone text for Gestalt learning theory.

18.4.2. Insight Learning

Köhler's chimps were presented with problems: for instance, bananas hung from the ceiling, with boxes scattered around. The chimps sometimes engaged in trial-and-error, but on certain occasions, they abruptly seemed to realize a solution—stacking boxes to climb on or joining two sticks to reach the fruit. This sudden reorganization of behavior illustrated **"insight learning"**:

1. **Perception of the Problem**: The chimp observes the environment, sees the fruit's placement, scans available tools (sticks, boxes).

2. **Sudden Restructuring**: At some moment, the chimp "perceives" the relation between the boxes or sticks and the goal.
3. **Solution**: The chimp systematically executes the discovered solution (building a platform, using a stick extension, etc.), typically with minimal errors.

Köhler argued that insight is not just the summation of previous S-R connections or random trial-and-error. Rather, the animal (or human) sees a new relationship among elements—**a Gestalt shift**—leading to immediate success. This phenomenon contradicted the strict behaviorist assumption that learning occurs incrementally, reinforced step by step. Instead, it suggested an **internal reorganization** of perception or cognition.

18.4.3. Implications for Learning Theory

Köhler's findings resonated with the broader Gestalt claim that the mind actively interprets contexts. If a situation's elements can be reorganized to reveal a solution, that shift can happen relatively suddenly, akin to the "Aha!" moment in human problem-solving. This perspective challenged the notion that all learning must be piecemeal shaping or associations.

While some critics argued that the apes might have previously learned box-stacking or stick-joining through incremental experiences, Köhler's descriptions illustrated a pattern that seemed more qualitative: the solution didn't appear partial or gradually reinforced but rather emerged after a period of exploration, often in a flash. This theme influenced later research on creative insight in humans, supporting the idea that problem-solving might sometimes rely on sudden reorganizations or new ways of seeing a problem.

18.5. Broader Concepts and Applications

18.5.1. Productive Thinking (Wertheimer)

Max Wertheimer extended Gestalt principles to **thinking** and **education**. In his book **Productive Thinking** (published posthumously in 1945), he distinguished **productive** from **reproductive** thinking:

- **Reproductive Thinking**: Applying familiar solutions by rote or mechanical formulas, akin to memorized responses.
- **Productive Thinking**: Restructuring a problem to see deeper insights, relationships, or principles—a truly creative process.

Wertheimer contended that genuine understanding arises when learners grasp the underlying relationships in a problem, not just external rules. He criticized teaching methods that rely on drills and memorization, urging approaches that help students see **structural patterns**. This notion mirrored the Gestalt emphasis on wholes and the significance of reorganizing one's mental representation to achieve clarity.

18.5.2. Gestalt and Social Psychology

Kurt Lewin (1890–1947), though not one of the original triumvirate, was heavily influenced by Gestalt ideas. He applied their holistic approach to **social psychology**, analyzing how individuals perceive their "life space" (the psychological environment of goals, barriers, and tensions).

Lewin's field theory posited that behavior is a function of the person and their environment, but conceptualized environment in a Gestalt-like manner—**patterns of group belonging, interpersonal forces, and perceived possibilities**. This orientation shaped group dynamics research and advanced the principle that social contexts are not sums of individuals but complex structures that must be understood as wholes.

18.6. Comparing Gestalt Psychology with Behaviorism

While Behaviorism gained prominence in the U.S., Gestalt Psychology thrived among certain intellectual circles. The two schools diverged sharply:

1. **Subject Matter**:
   - **Behaviorists**: Observable behavior, ignoring or downplaying mental events.
   - **Gestaltists**: Conscious experience, especially perception and meaning-making, regarded as vital for understanding the mind's organization.
2. **Method**:
   - **Behaviorists**: Laboratory measurement of stimuli and responses, often using animals.
   - **Gestaltists**: Experimental demonstrations of perceptual illusions, patterns, and problem-solving tasks; they used introspective reports to show how experiences shift qualitatively, combined with objective measures.
3. **Explanatory Focus**:
   - **Behaviorists**: Learning is incremental, based on reinforcement or punishment.
   - **Gestaltists**: Insightful reorganization, holistic pattern detection, with minimal emphasis on direct reinforcement.
4. **Philosophy**:
   - **Behaviorists**: Positivism, environmental determinism.
   - **Gestaltists**: Phenomenology, innate organizing tendencies of the mind.

These differences meant that, though both schools considered themselves scientific, they targeted different phenomena with distinct methods. By mid-century, Behaviorism overshadowed Gestalt in many American departments, but Gestalt principles remained crucial in perception research and reemerged strongly with the later cognitive revolution.

18.7. Critiques and Limitations

18.7.1. Overemphasis on Perception

Critics argued that Gestalt psychology focused too heavily on visual perception and illusions, neglecting other domains such as learning in everyday contexts, social behavior, and complex cognition. While Gestaltists did apply their framework to learning (especially Köhler's apes), the majority of their influential demonstrations involved perceptual grouping or ambiguous figures.

Moreover, some philosophers questioned whether illusions like the phi phenomenon truly refuted earlier views or whether they could be explained by simpler sensorimotor processes. Gestaltists insisted that the illusions reflected fundamental, irreducible properties of holistic perception.

18.7.2. Lack of Detailed Mechanisms

Behaviorists criticized Gestalt psychology for describing how the mind organizes stimuli without providing **mechanistic** explanations. Gestaltists used terms like "field forces" or "isomorphism" (the idea that brain activity mirrors perceptual wholes), but they rarely provided precise neural or algorithmic accounts.

Köhler attempted to connect Gestalt patterns to electromagnetic fields in the cortex, but these speculations lacked concrete physiological evidence at the time. As neuroscience advanced, some saw potential correlations (e.g., distributed neural networks forming global patterns), but Gestalt theories had limited direct testing in the lab beyond demonstrations of illusions and problem-solving tasks.

18.7.3. Historical Constraints

With the forced emigration of key Gestalt figures and the overshadowing influence of Behaviorism in the U.S., the Gestalt movement did not flourish institutionally. Funding, labs, and strong networks favored behaviorist or functionalist approaches. Over time, Gestalt psychology was partly absorbed into mainstream cognition research, losing its identity as a separate "school."

Nonetheless, the notion that the mind spontaneously forms coherent wholes strongly influenced future approaches in cognitive psychology, especially in areas like pattern recognition, object perception, and memory organization (schema theory). The intellectual seeds planted by Gestalt thinkers found new life decades later in the cognitive revolution, albeit framed in more computational or information-processing terms.

18.8. Lasting Contributions

Despite challenges, Gestalt psychology contributed lasting insights to psychology:

1. **Holistic Perception**: The demonstration that perception is not simply the summation of sensory elements but arises from pattern organization. Modern research on visual illusions, figure-ground segregation, and object recognition still relies on Gestalt principles.
2. **Insights into Learning and Creativity**: Köhler's "Aha!" experiments introduced the idea of **insight** as a sudden reorganization of mental structures. This concept remains

relevant in studies of creativity, brainstorming, and problem-solving.
3. **Principles of Organization**: The rules (similarity, proximity, closure, continuity, etc.) are taught in design, art, architecture, and human-computer interaction to ensure that visual displays match how humans group and interpret data.
4. **Influence on Cognitive Psychology**: Gestalt emphasis on the active mind, structure, and meaning laid groundwork for the shift away from purely behaviorist S-R analyses. In the mid-20th century, some cognitive psychologists revived Gestalt concepts to explore mental representations, schemas, and pattern matching.

18.9. Gestalt Psychology in the Wider Intellectual Landscape

Gestalt theory also impacted philosophy, art, and design. Artists exploring abstract forms leveraged Gestalt principles to create illusions of depth or unity. Designers used alignment, proximity, and closure to ensure visual clarity. In architecture, visual grouping and symmetry guided how spaces evoke certain emotional or aesthetic responses.

German philosophers, such as Ernst Cassirer, drew parallels between Gestalt thinking and symbolic forms in culture, arguing that humans interpret reality through structured categories. Even some psychoanalysts (e.g., Fritz Perls, who developed Gestalt therapy) borrowed the term "Gestalt" to stress holistic awareness of the present moment, though Gestalt therapy differed significantly from classical Gestalt psychology's experimental roots.

CHAPTER 19: EARLY 20TH CENTURY DEBATES AND DEVELOPMENTS

19.1. Introduction

By the first decades of the 20th century, the field of psychology had splintered into multiple competing perspectives. **Structuralism** (led by Edward Titchener in the United States) still clung to introspection. **Functionalism** (inspired by William James) took a broader, more pragmatic view of mental processes. **Behaviorism**, championed by John B. Watson, insisted that only measurable, observable behavior should form psychology's subject matter. In Europe, **Psychoanalysis** (Sigmund Freud and his circle) explored the unconscious mind and repressed desires, while **Gestalt Psychology** (Wertheimer, Koffka, Köhler) emphasized holistic perception and sudden insight.

This pluralism ignited fervent debates about psychology's proper methods, objects of study, and theoretical frameworks. Some observers predicted that one school would prevail and unify the discipline, while others saw permanent fragmentation ahead. Yet amid these controversies, new subfields started to take shape—personality assessment, psychometrics, intelligence testing, comparative psychology, industrial/organizational psychology, and the psychology of mental health. Universities expanded their psychology departments, and specialized journals multiplied.

In this chapter, we examine the **interplay and tensions** among the major schools, highlighting how they influenced each other's ideas and methods. We then explore emerging trends in personality theory, mental testing, child guidance, and industrial applications. Even as Behaviorism and Psychoanalysis each gained large followings, many psychologists found themselves in more eclectic positions, integrating bits from different traditions. We see how the early 20th century laid the groundwork for mid-century transformations, while still remaining in the historical realm prior to major post-World War II shifts.

19.2. Contested Boundaries

19.2.1. Increasing Specialization

The early 1900s saw psychology departments grow in North America and Europe. Harvard, Columbia, Chicago, Yale, and other institutions expanded labs for experimental work and offered graduate training in multiple approaches. But the curriculum varied widely: some programs emphasized introspective methods (Structuralism) or philosophical underpinnings, while others taught rigorous behaviorist experiments with animals or engaged with psychoanalytic theories of the unconscious.

As the discipline fractured, specialized journals arose:

- **Journal of Abnormal Psychology** (founded 1906) dedicated to psychopathology.
- **Journal of Educational Psychology** (founded 1910) reflecting interest in applying psychological principles to schooling.
- **Psychological Monographs** (various topics) and specialized outlets for psychometrics or comparative studies.

This proliferation was both a sign of vitality and a challenge to unity. Could introspective lab work, psychoanalytic case studies, child development observations, and rat-learning experiments all fit under one scientific umbrella? Many debated whether they shared a common core or were diverging into incompatible directions.

19.2.2. American Psychological Association and Other Societies

In the United States, the **American Psychological Association (APA)**—founded in 1892—served as a national forum, but it too reflected the discipline's diversity. Meetings featured presentations on perception experiments, intelligence tests, psychoanalytic theories, and more. Attempts to set universal research standards foundered on disagreements about method (introspection vs. observation vs. clinical case analysis).

In Europe, psychoanalytic societies formed around Freud, Jung, Adler, and others, while separate national societies of experimental psychology (often connected to physiology or philosophy departments) upheld different traditions. The Gestalt group rarely joined the mainstream associations wholeheartedly, preferring their own networks. Meanwhile, the British Psychological Society (founded 1901) grappled with balancing scientific and clinical interests. These parallel institutions mirrored the theoretical schisms playing out in print and at conferences.

19.3. Expanding Applications

19.3.1. Binet, Simon, and the First Intelligence Scales

One of the most influential early 20th-century developments was the **practical measurement** of individual differences. While Behaviorists might view mental constructs with suspicion, other psychologists sought to quantify abilities such as intelligence, memory, and reasoning in systematic ways.

In France, **Alfred Binet (1857–1911)** and **Théodore Simon (1873–1961)** developed the first modern intelligence test around 1905, commissioned by the French government to identify children in need of special education. Their test included items measuring memory, vocabulary, problem-solving, and judgment. Binet introduced the concept of **mental age**, comparing a child's performance to the average for their chronological age group.

This approach parted ways with introspection or psychoanalysis, focusing on direct task performance. Binet believed intelligence was multifaceted and malleable, cautioning against seeing his test as a fixed measure of innate capacity. Still, the test's success in practical settings inspired psychologists worldwide to refine and expand intelligence testing.

19.3.2. Goddard, Terman, and the IQ Concept

In the United States, **Henry H. Goddard** introduced the Binet-Simon scales to American schools, adopting them to identify "feeble-minded" children. Goddard's work, however, became entangled with eugenics movements, as he advocated segregating individuals with low scores. Meanwhile, **Lewis Terman (1877–1956)** at Stanford University revised the scale into the "Stanford-Binet," coining the **intelligence quotient (IQ)** as the ratio of mental age to chronological age multiplied by 100. The Stanford-Binet test set a precedent for intelligence testing in the U.S., widely used in schools and institutions.

Terman's large-scale studies (e.g., on gifted children) framed intelligence as relatively stable and measurable, though critics questioned cultural biases in test items. Still, the success of these scales in predicting academic performance spurred further psychometric research, forging a new subdiscipline of **quantitative psychology**. Tools like factor analysis would soon be developed by Charles Spearman in England, revealing potential underlying constructs (g factor) that might drive performance across many cognitive tasks.

19.3.3. Yerkes and Army Testing

World War I (1914–1918) also accelerated mental testing. The U.S. Army asked **Robert Yerkes (1876–1956)** and colleagues to devise group intelligence tests for recruits—**Army Alpha and Army Beta**—hoping to classify soldiers quickly. These large-scale assessments bolstered the credibility of psychometrics as a practical tool. Although the tests faced criticisms for cultural bias (favoring those with familiarity with English and formal schooling), the mere act of testing thousands of recruits advanced the idea that standardized psychological measures could inform institutional decisions.

After the war, many psychologists found opportunities in educational, corporate, or clinical settings, administering or creating tests for intelligence, aptitude, personality, and more. Even though Behaviorists might question the concept of "intelligence" as an internal trait, psychometricians pressed on with data-driven approaches, aligning with Functionalist ideals of practical utility.

19.4. Personality Assessment and Early Trait Theories

19.4.1. Woodworth's Personal Data Sheet

As the impetus to measure individual characteristics grew, attempts to quantify personality soon followed. During World War I, **Robert S. Woodworth** created a "Personal Data Sheet" to screen soldiers for susceptibility to "shell shock" (war neurosis). This questionnaire asked about nervous symptoms, worries, phobias, and personal habits. Though rudimentary by later standards, it was among the first structured self-report personality inventories, signaling a shift toward measuring traits or tendencies systematically rather than relying solely on clinical interviews or psychoanalytic interpretation.

19.4.2. Allport's and Early Trait Perspectives

Gordon Allport (1897–1967) emerged as a key figure in American personality psychology. While still a graduate student in the early 1920s, Allport visited Freud, an encounter that left him wary of overemphasizing unconscious motives. Instead, he championed a **trait** approach, focusing on how consistent patterns of thought, feeling, and behavior define an individual.

Allport worked on classifying traits by sifting through the dictionary for descriptive terms. Although his major theoretical contributions came slightly later, the seeds were planted in this early period. He encouraged an eclectic approach, acknowledging the influence of learning, biology, and internal motivations, bridging some gaps between Behaviorism and psychoanalytic or introspective viewpoints. Allport's early writings paved the way for further trait-based theories, though full-blown trait psychology would not flourish until mid-century.

19.5. Child Guidance, Clinical Practice, and the Mental Hygiene Movement

19.5.1. Emergence of Child Guidance Clinics

As mental testing and psychoanalytic ideas spread, many reformers sought to address childhood mental or emotional difficulties before they hardened into adult pathologies. **Child guidance clinics** appeared in major cities, often staffed by a psychologist, social worker, and psychiatrist. They assessed children's intelligence, emotional development, and family situations, aiming to intervene early with therapy, counseling, or special education.

This new orientation meshed with Progressive Era ideals: the belief that social and scientific methods could prevent delinquency and mental illness. Clinicians drew selectively on psychoanalysis (emphasizing early experiences), intelligence testing (for academic placement), and social work. The practical synergy contrasted with academic rivalries, showing how, in applied settings, multiple psychological paradigms might coexist for practical ends.

19.5.2. Clifford Beers and Mental Hygiene

A parallel movement called **Mental Hygiene** took shape in the early 1900s, spearheaded by Clifford Beers, who wrote an influential autobiographical account A Mind That Found Itself (1908). Beers described his experiences in mental institutions, advocating humane treatment, early intervention, and public education about mental health.

Prominent psychologists and psychiatrists joined the cause, leading to the formation of the **National Committee for Mental Hygiene** in the U.S. (1909). While not bound to a single theoretical stance, the mental hygiene movement highlighted the rising public awareness of psychological well-being, the possibility of prevention, and the role of scientific psychology in shaping public policy. The involvement of prominent figures like William James and Adolf Meyer indicated a shift toward more integrated approaches than strict theoretical camps.

19.6. Neo-Freudians and Other Psychoanalytic Splinters

19.6.1. Beyond Freud: Horney, Fromm, and Sullivan

Even as Freudian psychoanalysis gained worldwide attention, various **neo-Freudians** modified or diverged from Freud's original doctrines.

Unlike Jung and Adler, who broke away in the early years, these later analysts remained nominally within the psychoanalytic tradition but emphasized cultural, social, and interpersonal factors as much as unconscious drives.

1. **Karen Horney (1885–1952)**: A German physician who immigrated to the U.S., Horney challenged Freud's views on female psychology (e.g., "penis envy"), arguing that cultural influences shaped women's sense of inferiority. She also proposed that basic anxiety stemming from childhood helplessness drives people to develop neurotic strategies like compliance, aggression, or detachment.
2. **Erich Fromm (1900–1980)**: Fromm combined psychoanalysis with sociology and philosophy, focusing on how economic and cultural systems affect human needs for freedom, security, and belonging.
3. **Harry Stack Sullivan (1892–1949)**: An American psychiatrist, Sullivan emphasized **interpersonal relations**, seeing personality as shaped by interactions and the dynamism of social experiences.

Though much of their major work extends beyond our pre-mid-20th-century timeframe, the seeds were planted in the early 1920s and 1930s. These neo-Freudians introduced more emphasis on social context and relationships, broadening psychoanalytic discourse beyond sexual and aggressive drives.

19.6.2. Psychodynamic Tensions

Freud himself grew increasingly dogmatic about the libido theory and the importance of early sexual conflicts. Meanwhile, younger analysts saw potential expansions or alternative focuses. Disputes about religion, culture, or gender roles sometimes led to rifts within psychoanalytic societies. Still, psychoanalysis retained a powerful hold on the European and, increasingly, American clinical establishment. Many psychiatrists integrated basic Freudian concepts into their practice, even if they leaned toward more moderate interpretations.

19.7. Behaviorism's Rise and Challenges in the 1920s and 1930s

19.7.1. The Influence of Watson and Shifting Public Attitudes

John B. Watson's flamboyant promotion of Behaviorism, along with its practical successes in education and advertising, boosted its popularity during the 1920s. Universities founded new labs focusing on animal learning, reinforcement, and stimulus-response analysis. Watson's experiments with "Little Albert" and his prescriptions for child-rearing (a systematic, almost mechanical approach) intrigued the public.

Yet some psychologists found pure Behaviorism reductive. **Edward Tolman** advanced a "cognitive behaviorist" approach, positing that rats developed internal "cognitive maps" of mazes, not merely sequences of S-R associations. **Clark L. Hull** proposed a more theoretical model with intervening variables such as drive and habit strength. These developments indicated an undercurrent that S-R formulas alone might not suffice, hinting at the eventual turn to more mentalistic constructs.

19.7.2. Industrial and Organizational Psychology

Even as mainstream Behaviorism focused on laboratory tasks, a practical offshoot emerged in **Industrial and Organizational (I/O) psychology**. Psychologists like **Walter Dill Scott** and **Hugo Münsterberg** applied behavioral principles to worker productivity, personnel selection, and consumer behavior. Behaviorist assumptions that environment shapes habits dovetailed with business needs to train employees efficiently, design effective work routines, and market products persuasively.

The 1920s also saw the **Hawthorne Studies** at Western Electric (though not purely behaviorist), which found that worker productivity changed due to social factors and attention from researchers—revealing complexities that simple S-R approaches might underestimate. Still, the infiltration of behaviorist logic into management influenced staff training and reward systems, illustrating how, in applied settings, partial acceptance of behaviorist principles could be harnessed for real-world outcomes.

19.8. Gestalt vs. Behaviorism and the European Influence

19.8.1. Gestalt in the U.S.: A Small But Vocal Community

With Wertheimer, Koffka, and Köhler in the United States by the 1930s (due to political upheaval in Germany), **Gestalt Psychology** gained some foothold in American universities. They gave lectures, published in English, and ran demonstration experiments on perception. Köhler's presence at Swarthmore College attracted students interested in holistic approaches.

However, Behaviorism's institutional dominance limited Gestalt's expansion. Many American graduate students found the Gestalt emphasis on consciousness and phenomenological descriptions at odds with the demand for objective, quantitative methods. Still, Gestalt's demonstrations of illusions and insight learning stirred interest among those dissatisfied with purely mechanistic S-R accounts.

19.8.2. Lewin's Field Theory and Social Psychology

Kurt Lewin, closely aligned with Gestalt principles, began applying field theory to social and developmental contexts. He insisted that group dynamics, leadership styles, and personal motivation could be analyzed as structured wholes. In the 1930s, Lewin's investigations of leadership climates (authoritarian, democratic, laissez-faire) on children's behavior exemplified an experimental approach that transcended Behaviorism's narrower lens.

Lewin and his students showed that the style of leadership changes the "social field" in which children operate, altering group morale and creativity—phenomena not easily reduced to simple S-R contingencies. This line of research signaled the potential synergy between Gestalt's holistic viewpoint and emerging social-psychological methods, forging a distinct identity for social psychology that integrated environment, group factors, and individual perception.

19.9. Intellectual Crosscurrents and Cross-Fertilization

19.9.1. Philosophical Pragmatism and Psychology

American philosophers like **John Dewey** and **George Herbert Mead** (affiliated with the Chicago school) championed **pragmatism**, emphasizing that ideas and theories should be evaluated by their practical consequences. This mindset supported functionalist or behaviorist inclinations, focusing on how the mind adapts to real-world demands and how knowledge can serve societal progress. Pragmatism also subtly encouraged tolerance of multiple methods—whatever worked best for a specific aim.

Thus, in the U.S., academic psychology drifted from pure theoretical disputes into solution-oriented research. Even psychoanalysis found some pragmatic acceptance when it showed results in clinical practice. Introspection, less obviously beneficial, receded in many institutions, though Titchener's influence lingered in a few strongholds.

19.9.2. European Émigrés and Their Impacts

Political turmoil in Europe (World War I, rise of fascism, Nazi persecution) drove many intellectuals to the U.S. in the 1920s and 1930s. Alongside Gestalt founders, other notable psychologists emigrated, bringing new methods or bridging traditions. For instance:

- **Jean Piaget**'s early works on child cognition, although based in Switzerland, circulated among English-speaking psychologists, hinting at a stage-like approach to learning distinct from either Behaviorism or psychoanalysis (though Piaget's major influence grew post-WWII).
- **Lev Vygotsky** in the Soviet Union (though less known internationally at this stage) developed a sociocultural approach to thought and language, with partial translation into Western discourse only beginning.

While the full impact of these figures would appear later, seeds of cross-fertilization were sown in the early 20th century as manuscripts, lectures, and translations introduced fresh perspectives.

19.10. The Shifting Landscape by the 1930s

19.10.1. Structuralism's Decline

Edward Titchener's Structuralism, which once rivaled other schools, gradually lost momentum. Titchener himself maintained a dedicated group of students, but the methodical introspective analysis of "mental elements" seemed increasingly outdated. Behaviorists disavowed introspection as unscientific; psychoanalysts insisted that much of mental life was unconscious and inaccessible to introspection anyway; functionalists considered Titchener's approach too narrow and impractical.

After Titchener's death in 1927, Structuralism all but dissolved as an organized force. A few labs carried on introspective procedures, but the mainstream had shifted toward Behaviorism or more eclectic approaches. Reflecting on Titchener's passing, some psychologists declared the end of an era—no single "golden thread" replaced it, but the discipline moved on, forging new lines of inquiry.

19.10.2. Psychoanalysis Gains Ground in Clinics

While mainstream academic psychology in the U.S. favored Behaviorism, **psychoanalytic** ideas steadily gained influence in clinical circles. Many psychiatrists (including those trained in Europe or exposed to Freudian concepts) established private practices, offering psychoanalysis or psychoanalytically informed therapy. Medical institutions recognized psychoanalysis as a potential approach to neurosis or hysteria, though controversies remained about its efficacy and scientific basis.

By the early 1930s, New York, Boston, and Chicago each had active psychoanalytic institutes. They taught budding psychiatrists, published clinical case reports, and cultivated a culture of "depth psychology" separate from the university-based labs. Tensions lingered between academically oriented psychologists (who demanded controlled experiments) and psychoanalysts (who insisted that the complexity of the unconscious demanded lengthy case studies). But the public fascination with Freud's ideas—plus patient testimonials—helped psychoanalysis secure a foothold in mental health care.

19.10.3. Behaviorism's Dominance in Experimental Psychology

In contrast, the majority of **experimental** psychology graduate programs, particularly in the American Midwest and West Coast, adopted Behaviorism or some variant. Journals such as the **Journal of Comparative Psychology** and **Journal of Experimental Psychology** published endless studies on animal learning, reinforcement schedules, and stimulus generalization.

- **Edward C. Tolman** introduced cognitivist elements but still framed them within a behavioral methodology.
- **Clark Hull** developed a complex set of postulates linking drives, reinforcement, and habit strength.
- **B.F. Skinner**, by the late 1930s, was elaborating his operant conditioning framework, though his major impact would come in subsequent decades.

This environment overshadowed Gestalt or psychoanalytic approaches in many academic departments. Yet critiques persisted: some argued that Behaviorism, while successful in controlling behavior in labs, failed to address real-life complexities (language, thought, culture). Nonetheless, as the 1930s came to a close, Behaviorism reigned supreme in academic experimental research.

19.11. War, Social Issues, and Psychology's Role

19.11.1. The Interwar Period and European Crises

The aftermath of World War I left many countries grappling with mass trauma, physical rehabilitation, and reintegration of veterans. Psychologists assisted in vocational guidance, intelligence and aptitude testing for job placement, and emotional support. In Europe, psychoanalysts were active in treating war neuroses. Behaviorists contributed to theories on retraining and habit re-formation for veterans.

Meanwhile, economic downturns (the Great Depression in the U.S., postwar inflation in Germany) spurred interest in how psychological research might address unemployment, mental stress, and social upheaval. Still, the discipline lacked a unified direction: Behaviorists offered environmental manipulation, psychoanalysts probed underlying conflicts, while others took a more pragmatic, interdisciplinary approach, blending psychological insight with social policy.

19.11.2. Growing Social Psychology

In the U.S. and Britain, social psychology began carving out a clearer identity. Lewin's group studied group dynamics, prejudice, leadership, and motivation. **Muzafer Sherif**, who had studied in Turkey and the U.S., developed experimental designs for understanding social norms (the autokinetic effect). Others, such as **Floyd Allport**, advanced a more individualistic approach, applying behaviorist or experimental methods to social questions (e.g., attitude formation, imitation).

This diversification showed that psychology was addressing broader societal issues: prejudice, conflict, persuasion, propaganda. The looming threat of another war in Europe (ultimately breaking out in 1939) furthered interest in how group processes and propaganda shape minds—foreshadowing more intense social-psychological research during and after World War II.

CHAPTER 20: BRIDGING TO THE MID-20TH CENTURY

20.1. Introduction

By the late 1930s and early 1940s, psychology had firmly established itself as an academic discipline and a profession. In universities, specialized laboratories investigated learning, perception, and cognition under varying theoretical banners—Behaviorist, Gestalt, or eclectic. Outside academia, clinical and applied psychologists tackled mental health, child guidance, intelligence testing, and industrial efficiency. The discipline was recognized worldwide, with numerous journals, associations, and conferences.

At the same time, the world was on the brink of cataclysmic events that would reshape societies and scientific priorities. Economic crises and political tensions in Europe, culminating in World War II (1939–1945), forced many scholars to emigrate. These upheavals further disseminated ideas across borders. Meanwhile, theoretical debates raged over whether psychology could unify around a single paradigm or whether the discipline would always harbor plural perspectives.

In this final chapter, we explore how the early 20th-century achievements, debates, and challenges **set the stage** for transformations that would occur by the mid-20th century—namely the expansions in clinical psychology, new conceptions of personality, continuing controversies around behaviorism vs. mentalism, and the beginnings of more sophisticated research into cognition. We remain within our historical timeframe, tracing only the **seeds** of these future changes, without delving fully into post-war or late 20th-century developments. This chapter thus marks a bridging point: psychology stands ready for further revolutions, but those lie just beyond the historical scope of our narrative.

20.2. The Impact of World War II Looming

20.2.1. Emigration, Brain Drain, and Cultural Exchange

Throughout the 1930s, as Nazi power rose in Germany, many Jewish psychologists—among them Gestalt theorists, psychoanalysts, and researchers in various subfields—fled to Britain or the United States. This diaspora spread ideas that might otherwise have remained localized in European contexts. American universities benefited from the influx of brilliant minds, but the forced migration also dismantled thriving research communities in Europe.

Although the war had not yet begun in 1939, the political climate was clearly building toward conflict. Emigré psychologists found new homes, shaping developments in child psychology, social psychology, psychoanalysis, and even testing programs in America. Kurt Lewin's field theory, for example, gained broader traction after his move to the U.S. Meanwhile, in Britain, psychoanalysis continued to expand, with figures like Anna Freud (Sigmund's daughter) and Melanie Klein deepening child psychoanalytic theory.

20.2.2. Preparation for Psychological Services

Anticipating large-scale social and military demands, psychologists in the late 1930s began discussing how psychological knowledge could serve national defense. Testing recruits, treating potential "battle neuroses," training officers, boosting morale—these tasks would require clinically and experimentally trained psychologists.

Organizations like the APA started forming committees to coordinate these efforts. The memory of World War I's testing programs and shell shock treatment indicated that psychology could play a key role.

Though not yet at the scale that would emerge once the war fully erupted, these early preparations signaled a shift from purely academic concerns to urgent applied demands. This emphasis on practical contributions, combined with existing trends in mental testing, industrial psychology, and therapy, suggested that after the war, psychology might expand into areas previously dominated by psychiatry or social work.

20.3. The Continued Divergence of Clinical and Experimental Psychology

20.3.1. Clinical Psychology's Growing Confidence

Clinical psychology—once a minor part of the field—expanded in the 1930s. Child guidance clinics, mental hygiene campaigns, and the rising popularity of psychoanalysis (or psychoanalytic-inspired therapy) boosted the profession. Although psychiatrists (with medical training) often wielded more authority in mental health settings, psychologists began carving out roles in assessment (e.g., intelligence or personality testing) and psychotherapy, sometimes in conjunction with psychiatrists.

Journals like the *Journal of Clinical Psychology* (founded later in the 1940s, but planned in this period) signaled professional recognition. University programs added clinical tracks that combined some psychoanalytic or dynamic theory with testing, though few integrated behaviorist approaches for clinical work—Behaviorism was typically relegated to the experimental lab. This schism between an experimental "lab-based" psychology and a "clinical/therapeutic" psychology deepened, though a minority of psychologists believed in bridging the two.

20.3.2. Varied Therapeutic Approaches

Even within clinical psychology, approaches diverged. Some psychologists were heavily influenced by psychoanalysis (Freudian, Jungian, or Adlerian). Others took a more pragmatic or "directive" approach, focusing on direct guidance or counseling techniques. A few began experimenting with "behavior therapy" ideas—though not systematically recognized under that name yet—using reinforcement to alter maladaptive habits.

At the institutional level, psychiatrists often overshadowed psychologists, relegating them to test administration. Still, psychologists found that their test data (IQ scores, projective tests like Rorschach or TAT) were in high demand. This gave them a foothold in hospital and clinic teams. The seeds for future expansion of clinical psychology were thus planted: a combination of psychoanalytic influences, psychometric tools, and some nascent behavior modification techniques.

20.4. Personality and Social Theories on the Horizon

20.4.1. The Emergence of Personality Theorists

By the 1930s, interest in systematic **personality theory** was rising. Gordon Allport's early trait approach, Henry Murray's personology (focused on needs and motives), and attempts to unify psychoanalysis with test-based research took shape. Murray, for instance, developed the **Thematic Apperception Test (TAT)**, which asked individuals to interpret ambiguous pictures, presumably revealing underlying motives and conflicts.

While these lines were still overshadowed by the big controversies—Behaviorism vs. Psychoanalysis—personality research quietly expanded. Some academics tried to incorporate quantitative trait methods with psychoanalytic ideas about deeper motives. For example, the TAT reflected both a projective method (similar to Rorschach's inkblot test) and a desire to code outcomes systematically. These bridging attempts indicated that the rigid boundaries between schools might soften over time, at least in the realm of personality assessment.

20.4.2. Social Psychology's Complexity

Lewin's influence, plus the intellectual climate in Europe, spurred more sophisticated studies of attitudes, group norms, leadership styles, and intergroup relations. Scholars like **Gordon Allport** (also a social psychologist) and **Floyd Allport** studied prejudice formation and group interactions. The 1930s saw emergent research on persuasion and propaganda, relevant to rising political movements in Europe.

While Behaviorism provided methods for measuring overt changes in attitudes (questionnaire responses, approach-avoidance behaviors), many social psychologists found purely S-R accounts inadequate. They invoked constructs like internal attitudes, field forces, or group climates—some influenced by Gestalt thinking. This tension foreshadowed a more explicit cognitive turn in social psychology after the war, but in the 1930s it remained overshadowed by behaviorist orthodoxy in most lab-based contexts.

20.5. Methodological Advances

20.5.1. Experimental Control and Factor Analysis

The 1920s and 1930s brought refinements in experimental **design** (e.g., the use of control groups, random assignment, double-blind procedures) to ensure reliability and validity. Psychologists sought to replicate the rigor of the natural sciences. Behaviorists, with their controlled animal studies, exemplified one approach, but others also recognized the need for standardized protocols in testing or social experiments.

On the quantitative side, **factor analysis**—pioneered by **Charles Spearman** for intelligence research—began to be applied more broadly, including in personality trait studies and test development. L.L. Thurstone at the University of Chicago advanced multiple-factor solutions, challenging Spearman's single "g factor" notion. These statistical innovations allowed psychologists to parse complex data sets systematically, searching for underlying dimensions of ability or personality.

Though widely adopted in psychometrics, factor analysis exemplified a departure from Behaviorist or psychoanalytic frameworks: it was a purely mathematical technique, not wedded to a single theoretical stance. A test constructor might be behaviorist in orientation, yet still use factor analysis to glean structure from test results; or a trait psychologist might use it to identify clusters of correlated behaviors. This method-based cross-pollination somewhat softened the boundaries among schools.

20.5.2. Early Longitudinal and Developmental Studies

Additionally, the idea of **longitudinal research** to track changes over time gained traction. For instance, Terman's study of gifted children (the "Termites") started in 1921 and continued for decades, gathering data on intellectual and social outcomes. Although Terman's perspective was partly overshadowed by Behaviorism in academic labs, such long-term data collection shaped how psychologists thought about stability vs. change in intelligence or personality.

Other developmental researchers, such as Arnold Gesell, systematically observed infant motor and cognitive milestones, blending descriptive methods with attempts at standardization. This approach, though not purely Behaviorist or psychoanalytic, drew upon child study traditions dating back to James and Hall, fueling the continued growth of developmental psychology as an empirical subfield.

20.6. Debates Over Consciousness and Introspection

20.6.1. Is Consciousness Entirely Outmoded?

Despite Behaviorism's dominance in experimental circles, some researchers still believed **consciousness** deserved study. A few labs in Europe maintained illusions or introspection experiments, refining phenomenological methods. Even in the U.S., a handful of psychologists at certain universities clung to Titchener's structural approach or advanced "imageless thought" introspection from Oswald Külpe's Würzburg School.

Nevertheless, the mainstream in America either ignored consciousness or re-labeled it in more operational terms. For instance, if an experiment required subjective reports, researchers might treat them as **verbal behaviors** subject to stimulus control. Psychoanalysts, focusing on unconscious conflict, ironically kept the notion of consciousness alive in clinical contexts, albeit overshadowed by deeper impulses.

Thus, consciousness was not fully banished: it survived in corners of academia (perception labs, some introspective enthusiasts, certain clinical methods) but lacked the institutional support enjoyed by behaviorist frameworks. The seeds of a renewed interest in consciousness lay dormant, waiting for a later shift in mid-century or beyond.

20.6.2. Phenomenology in Europe

On the European continent, **phenomenological** traditions also lingered, particularly in Germany and Austria, influenced by philosophers like Edmund Husserl. A handful of psychologists interested in direct, subjective experience (like Gestalt and phenomenology) survived, though the Nazi regime stifled academic freedom. Some phenomenological psychologists fled or hid their research.

This overshadowed tradition would partially resurface post-WWII in forms of existential or humanistic psychology, but by the late 1930s it remained marginal and overshadowed by the exodus of talent and repressive political climate. Where it did exist, phenomenological psychology insisted on describing subjective lived experiences in detail, in direct contrast to behaviorist reliance on objective external measures.

20.7. The Growth of Professional Training and Associations

20.7.1. University Curricula

By the mid-1930s, many universities offered specialized courses in learning theory, abnormal psychology, child development, experimental design, and psychometrics. Master's and doctoral programs grew, and more young psychologists sought academic or applied careers. Behaviorist paradigms guided many lab-based courses, while psychoanalysis influenced clinical tracks.

In Europe, the fragmentation caused by rising authoritarian regimes disrupted academic continuity. Some institutions in Great Britain or neutral countries carried on multiple approaches, but German universities lost leading figures to exile. In the U.S., ironically, this meant an influx of new perspectives from émigrés, leading to more diverse graduate offerings.

20.7.2. APA's Evolving Structure

The American Psychological Association (APA) adapted to the expanding profession by creating divisions for different areas of practice and research: clinical, educational, industrial, etc. This attempt at organization recognized that a single set of methods or theories no longer covered all psychological endeavors.

Behaviorist-minded experimental psychologists often commanded editorial positions in top journals, shaping the discipline's "core," while psychoanalytic or clinical psychologists formed their own networks. The APA tried to unify them under one umbrella, but internal politics sometimes erupted over which perspective should set standards for publications or ethics. By the late 1930s, the APA included committees on ethics, testing standards, and training guidelines, foreshadowing future professionalization of psychology.

20.8. Seeds of Future Directions

20.8.1. Moves Toward Broader Cognition

Even as Behaviorism dominated, some in the late 1930s began to see limitations. Tolman's cognitive maps hinted at unseen processes guiding behavior. Gestalt psychologists studied problem-solving beyond mere reinforcement. Social psychologists confronted intangible constructs like attitudes, beliefs, norms.

Though still overshadowed, these nascent focuses on mental representation or internal structures set the stage for a more cognitive approach that would flourish after World War II. This upcoming shift was not yet a revolution, but pockets of interest in memory, language, and concept formation existed quietly.

20.8.2. War's Impending Influence on Research

The approaching war would demand solutions for morale, propaganda, leadership, selection, and training. Psychology's role would expand drastically, providing impetus for new experiments and interventions. Some see the war as a "great accelerator" for applied psychological science, leading to advanced testing programs, the study of human factors (e.g., pilot performance, instrument design), and the push for effective therapy for soldiers' trauma.

In addition, the war disrupted normal academic careers. Many psychologists joined the military or government agencies, applying their skills in intelligence, psychological warfare, or rehabilitation. This preludes a major transformation in how psychologists thought about measurement, group dynamics, communication, and mental health, but as of the late 1930s, these changes were only beginning.

20.9. Summation of the Pre-Mid-20th Century State

By the close of the 1930s and early 1940s:

1. **Behaviorism** was still the dominant force in American experimental psychology, claiming that objective observation of stimulus-response relationships was the essence of science. Yet critics and alternative viewpoints (Tolman's cognitive

inferences, Gestalt insights) hinted at underlying mental processes.
2. **Psychoanalysis** maintained strong clinical and cultural influence. Freudian thought, albeit in modified forms (neo-Freudians, child analysis), permeated mental health discourse, especially in Europe and urban U.S. centers. Disputes over sexuality, the unconscious, and repressed memories continued.
3. **Gestalt Psychology** introduced robust challenges to atomistic or purely S-R frameworks, emphasizing holistic perception and insight learning. Emigration to the U.S. disseminated Gestalt ideas, yet they never dominated American psychology.
4. **Psychometrics and Intelligence Testing** thrived in educational and industrial contexts. Large-scale testing programs validated the idea that psychological constructs like "intelligence" or "aptitude" could be measured reliably, driving the growth of quantitative methods.
5. **Clinical Psychology** was gaining self-confidence, bridging psychoanalytic methods, psychometrics, and a desire for professional recognition. Hospitals and clinics increasingly hired psychologists to test and assist patients, though psychiatrists still held ultimate authority in many settings.
6. **Social Psychology** emerged as a distinct domain, influenced by Gestalt principles (Lewin) and American experimental traditions. It investigated attitudes, group behavior, leadership, and social norms—foreshadowing its critical role in wartime propaganda studies and post-war expansions.
7. **Increasing Professionalization** with specialized divisions, journals, and ethical committees indicated that psychologists recognized themselves as a multifaceted but coherent discipline—though theoretical unity was elusive.

Thus, the stage was set for mid-century transformations, as the pressures of World War II and its aftermath would reshape priorities, funding, and intellectual climates. Although we do not venture into later developments, it is evident that the seeds of major revolutions—cognitive approaches, expanded clinical roles, advanced psychometrics, new social psychological paradigms—were already planted.

Conclusion

This final chapter completes our historical journey of psychology up to the threshold of the mid-20th century. We have traced how multiple schools coexisted, competed, and cross-fertilized: **Behaviorists** in the lab, **Psychoanalysts** in clinics, **Gestalt** theorists focusing on holistic perception, **Functionalists** offering practical solutions, and **psychometricians** measuring intelligence, personality, and aptitudes. Child guidance, industrial applications, and social concerns propelled the field beyond the ivory tower.

By the early 1940s, psychology was recognized as a mature, albeit fragmented, discipline. The events about to unfold—World War II, major expansions in government funding for research, the subsequent transformations in technology and intellectual thought—would lead to new waves of theoretical and methodological change, culminating in the mid-century expansions that we acknowledge but do not detail here. Our account ends at this critical juncture, with psychology poised to adapt and transform yet again, driven by social needs, scientific ambitions, and the cross-pollination of ideas inherited from these early decades.

www.ingramcontent.com/pod-product-compliance
Lightning Source LLC
LaVergne TN
LVHW012038070526
838202LV00056B/5535